The Theology of the Churches and the Jewish People

The Theology of the Churches and the Jewish People

Statements by the World Council of Churches and its member churches.

With a commentary by Allan Brockway, Paul van Buren, Rolf Rendtorff, Simon Schoon.

WCC Publications, Geneva

Cover design: Rob Lucas

ISBN 2-8254-0932-4

© 1988 WCC Publications, World Council of Churches,
150 route de Ferney, 1211 Geneva 20, Switzerland

Printed in Switzerland

Table of Contents

The Commentary

Preface

The official theology of Christian churches is not determined by theologians or the common belief of Christians but by decisions taken at synods, conventions, and assemblies by delegates chosen to represent the membership at large, including theologians. What does this official theology say about Jews and Judaism? And, perhaps even more important, what does it say about Christian faith itself — in light of what theologians, historians, and biblical scholars are saying and writing about the significance of the Jewish people for the faith of the church? The twenty statements by churches and church bodies that comprise the first part of this book, and the commentary that follows, are designed to offer some answers to these questions.

During its meeting at the Arnoldshain Evangelical Academy (Federal Republic of Germany) in February 1986, the World Council of Churches' Consultation on the Church and the Jewish People (CCJP [1]) resolved:

> It is now our aim to bring before the WCC and its member churches the fruits of Jewish-Christian dialogue over many years and in many lands. In that task we give priority to the need for distilling elements found in the various documents already accepted by various churches and by the WCC itself. We want so to present this material that the fundamental convergences there to be found can receive the widest hearing and acceptance possible in the oikoumene. We foresee a language with the power and simplicity the truth requires.

---

[1] The Consultation on the Church and the Jewish People is the successor to the International Missionary Council's Committee on the Christian Approach to the Jews. It is now elected by the working group of the WCC's Sub-unit on Dialogue with People of Living Faiths and is composed of Christians who are concerned for the Jewish people and for the theological integrity of the church.

Towards that end, the CCJP named a task force to examine carefully selected WCC and member-church statements on the Jewish people that have been issued since the founding of the World Council in 1948, from the perspective of the theology both explicit and implicit within them. The task force, chosen from the membership of the CCJP, was composed of Rolf Rendtorff (Federal Republic of Germany); Paul van Buren (United States of America); Simon Schoon (Netherlands); Theodore Stylianopoulos (United States of America); and Allan Brockway (Switzerland/USA), CCJP secretary. Christopher Duraisingh (India) withdrew with great regret because of schedule conflicts.

The pages that follow contain a selection of statements by the churches relative to Jews and Judaism. They are from two principal sources: the World Council of Churches and member churches of the World Council, the latter of which are solely from the so-called North Atlantic churches. It is not surprising that that should be so, for the history of the church's relation with and to the Jewish people largely has been written in Europe and, more recently, North America. That does not mean, of course, that churches in Asia, Africa and South America are unaware of the Jewish people or are unaffected by antisemitism. But it does mean that they have not, as official church bodies, taken theological positions relative to the Jewish people as their more northern co-religionists have. [2] The Orthodox family of churches also is not represented among the statements offered here. Nevertheless, though no Orthodox church has officially issued a statement on the Jewish people, to date three Orthodox-Jewish consultations have been held at the international level and another is planned.

Following the statements by the churches is a series of theological analyses written by four members of the CCJP task force, each of whom is responsible for the section identified by his initials: Rolf Rendtorff (RR), Paul van Buren (PvB), Simon Schoon (SSch), and Allan Brockway (AB). Theodore Stylianopoulos participated in several meetings of the task force and gave the authors the benefit of his theological thought and knowledge of the Orthodox churches. Kofi Opoku (Ghana) carefully evaluated the documents and the various drafts of the commentary and submitted observations that are reflected in the report. Åke Skoog (Israel/ Sweden) engaged the Ecumenical Theological Research Fraternity in Israel in the study, providing a stimulating evaluation of the various documents' positions on the State of Israel. And Biörn Fjärstedt (Sweden), moderator of the CCJP, offered invaluable advice and counsel in the

---

[2] See IV, "Final Reflections".

final redaction stages. However, only the four authors, individually and collectively, may be held accountable for what they have written.

This book is offered in the hope that churches throughout the world will continue to reflect on the significance of the Jewish people for their own faith and life and will undertake with greater vigour the theological re-evaluation that forty years of intentional dialogue with Jews has made incumbent upon us all.

The
Documents

I

Statements by the Churches

Introduction

The following selection of documents has two parts. The first part (A) is composed of statements and reports from the World Council of Churches concerning relations to Jews, Judaism, and the State of Israel, beginning with the First Assembly of the World Council at Amsterdam in 1948. [1] The second part (B) is a selection of similar statements, reports and studies from various member churches of the World Council.

The status of the individual documents is different. Five of the six Assemblies of the World Council passed formal resolutions on these issues (Amsterdam, 1948 [Doc. 1]; New Delhi, 1961 [Doc. 3]; Uppsala, 1968 [Doc. 5]; Nairobi, 1975 [Doc. 6]); and Vancouver, 1983 [Doc. 8]. At Evanston (1954) a section on "The Hope of Israel" was deleted from the proposed text of the statement on the main theme, which was "Jesus Christ: the Hope of the World", but a minority report (Doc. 2) was published as an appendix in the Assembly report.

In 1967 the Commission on Faith and Order accepted a report (Doc. 4) of the Committee (now Consultation) on the Church and the Jewish People or CCJP, which, however, was *not* brought before the Assembly. In 1982 the "Ecumenical Considerations on Jewish-Christian Dialogue" (Doc. 7), which had been developed over a seven-year period by the CCJP, was received by the Executive Committee of the WCC and "commended to the churches for study and action".

The second part of the collection (B) contains a selection of statements, reports, and studies from different member churches of the World

---

[1] Resolutions of the Provisional Committee of the World Council of Churches (in process of formation) from 1946 are also quoted in parts II and III.

Council. The great number of relevant documents made it impossible to include them all in this volume. Those included are intended to represent the most important positions, developments and trends among the churches that comprise the World Council; therefore the inclusion or omission of any given statement should not be taken as a judgment on its importance or value. [2]

In part B the status of the individual documents is, as in part A, different. Some of them are official statements by the highest bodies of the respective churches, such as synods, general conference, general conventions, and the like: (Evangelical Church in Germany 1950 [Doc. 9]; the Netherlands Reformed Church [Doc. 10]; United Methodist Church in the USA 1972 [Doc. 12]; American Lutheran Church 1974 [Doc. 13]; Evangelical Church of the Rhineland 1980 [Doc. 17]; Evangelical Church of Berlin (West) 1984 [Doc. 19]; Presbyterian Church (USA) 1987 [Doc. 20]).

Others are declarations by representatives or leadership of regional church conferences (Norway 1977 [Doc. 16]; Texas Conference of Churches 1982 [Doc. 18]).

A third group consists of studies carried out by a certain committee and adopted by the representative church body or leadership (Netherlands Reformed Church 1970 [Doc. 11]; Evangelical Church in Germany 1975 [Doc. 14]; and Swiss Protestant Church Federation 1977 [Doc. 15]).

---

[2] The same is true in those cases when only some parts of a more extensive document have been included.

The First Assembly
of the World Council of Churches

The Assembly, held at Amsterdam from 22 August to 4 September 1948, received the report of Committee IV "Concerns of the Churches" with its chapter 3, "The Christian Approach to the Jews".

Introduction

A concern for the Christian approach to the Jewish people confronts us inescapably, as we meet together to look with open and penitent eyes on man's disorder and to rediscover together God's eternal purpose for His Church. This concern is ours because it is first a concern of God made known to us in Christ. No people in His one world have suffered more bitterly from the disorder of man than the Jewish people. We cannot forget that we meet in a land from which 110,000 Jews were taken to be murdered. Nor can we forget that we meet only five years after the extermination of 6 million Jews. To the Jews our God has bound us in a special solidarity linking our destinies together in His design. We call upon all our churches to make this concern their own as we share with them the results of our too brief wrestling with it.

1. The Church's commission to preach the Gospel to all men

All of our churches stand under the commission of our common Lord, "Go ye into all the world and preach the Gospel to every creature." The fulfilment of this commission requires that we include the Jewish people in our evangelistic task.

2. The special meaning of the Jewish people for Christian faith

In the design of God, Israel has a unique position. It was Israel with whom God made His covenant by the call of Abraham. It was Israel to whom God revealed His name and gave His law. It was to Israel that He sent His Prophets with their message of judgment and of grace. It was Israel to whom He promised the coming of His Messiah. By the history of Israel God prepared the manger in which in the fullness of time He put the Redeemer of all mankind, Jesus Christ. The Church has received this spiritual heritage from Israel and is therefore in honour bound to render it back in the light of the Cross. We have, therefore, in humble conviction to proclaim to the Jews, "The Messiah for Whom you wait has come." The promise has been fulfilled by the coming of Jesus Christ.

For many the continued existence of a Jewish people which does not acknowledge Christ is a divine mystery which finds its only sufficient explanation in the purpose of God's unchanging faithfulness and mercy (Rom. 11:25-29).

3. Barriers to be overcome

Before our churches can hope to fulfill the commission laid upon us by our Lord there are high barriers to be overcome. We speak here particularly of the barriers which we have too often helped to build and which we alone can remove.

We must acknowledge in all humility that too often we have failed to manifest Christian love towards our Jewish neighbours, or even a resolute will for common social justice. We have failed to fight with all our strength the age-old disorder of man which anti-semitism represents. The churches in the past have helped to foster an image of the Jews as the sole enemies of Christ, which has contributed to anti-semitism in the secular world. In many lands virulent anti-semitism still threatens and in other lands the Jews are subjected to many indignities.

We call upon all the churches we represent to denounce anti-semitism, no matter what its origin, as absolutely irreconcilable with the profession and practice of the Christian faith. Anti-semitism is sin against God and man.

Only as we give convincing evidence to our Jewish neighbours that we seek for them the common rights and dignities which God wills for His children, can we come to such a meeting with them as would make it possible to share with them the best which God has given us in Christ.

4. The Christian witness to the Jewish people

In spite of the universality of our Lord's commission and of the fact that the first mission of the Church was to the Jewish people, our churches have with rare exceptions failed to maintain that mission. This responsibility should not be left largely to independent agencies. The carrying on of this mission by special agencies has often meant the singling out of the Jews for special missionary attention, even in situations where they might well have been included in the normal ministry of the church. It has also meant in many cases that the converts are forced into segregated spiritual fellowship rather than being included and welcomed in the regular membership of the church.

Owing to this failure our churches must consider the responsibility for missions to the Jews as a normal part of parish work, especially in those countries where Jews are members of the general community. Where there is no indigenous church or where the indigenous church is insufficient for this task it may be necessary to arrange for a special missionary ministry from abroad.

Because of the unique inheritance of the Jewish people, the churches should make provision for the education of ministers specially fitted for this task. Provision should also be made for Christian literature to interpret the gospel to Jewish people.

Equally, it should be made clear to church members that the strongest argument in winning others for Christ is the radiance and contagion of victorious living and the outgoing of God's love expressed in personal human contacts. As this is expressed and experienced in a genuine Christian fellowship and community the impact of the Gospel will be felt. For such a fellowship there will be no difference between a converted Jew and other church members, all belonging to the same church and fellowship through Jesus Christ. But the converted Jew calls for particular tenderness and full acceptance just because his coming into the church carries with it often a deeply wounding break with family and friends.

In reconstruction and relief activities the churches must not lose sight of the plight of Christians of Jewish origin, in view of their special suffering. Such provision must be made for their aid as will help them to know that they are not forgotten in the Christian fellowship.

5. The emergence of Israel as a state

The establishment of the state "Israel" adds a political dimension to the Christian approach to the Jews and threatens to complicate anti-semitism with political fears and enmities.

On the political aspects of the Palestine problem and the complex conflict of "rights" involved we do not undertake to express a judgment. Nevertheless, we appeal to the nations to deal with the problem not as one of expediency — political, strategic or economic — but as a moral and spiritual question that touches a nerve centre of the world's religious life.

Whatever position may be taken towards the establishment of a Jewish state and towards the "rights" and "wrongs" of Jews and Arabs, of Hebrew Christians and Arab Christians involved, the churches are in duty bound to pray and work for an order in Palestine as just as may be in the midst of our human disorder; to provide within their power for the relief of the victims of this warfare without discrimination; and to seek to influence the nations to provide a refuge for "Displaced Persons" far more generously than has yet been done.

Recommendations

We conclude this report with the recommendations which arise out of our first exploratory consideration of this "concern" of the churches.

1. To the member churches of the World Council we recommend:
— that they seek ro recover the universality of our Lord's commission by including the Jewish people in their evangelistic work;
— that they encourage their people to seek for brotherly contact with and understanding of their Jewish neighbours, and cooperation in agencies combating misunderstanding and prejudice;
— that in mission work among the Jews they scrupulously avoid all unworthy pressures or inducements;
— that they give thought to the preparation of ministers well fitted to interpret the Gospel to Jewish people and to the provision of literature which will aid in such a ministry.

2. To the World Council of Churches we recommend:
— that it should give careful thought as to how it can best stimulate and assist the member churches in the carrying out of this aspect of their mission;
— that it give careful consideration to the suggestion made by the International Missionary Council that the World Council of Churches share with it a joint responsibility for the Christian approach to the Jews;
— that it be resolved:
that, in receiving the report of this Committee, the Assembly recognize the need for more detailed study by the World Council of

Churches of the many complex problems which exist in the field of relations between Christians and Jews and in particular of the following:

(a) the historical and present factors which have contributed to the growth and persistence of anti-semitism, and the most effective means of combating this evil;

(b) the need and opportunity in this present historical situation for the development of cooperation between Christians and Jews in civic and social affairs;

(c) the many and varied problems created by establishment of a State of Israel in Palestine.

The Assembly therefore asks that these and related questions be referred to the Central Committee for further examination.

● From: *The First Assembly of the World Council of Churches*, official report, New York, Harper & Bros, 1949, pp.160-164.

The Second Assembly
of the World Council of Churches

The Assembly, held at Evanston from 15 to 31 August 1954, rejected to include a passage on the hope of Israel in its statement on "Christ our Hope". As a reaction to that decision a number of delegates issued a separate statement on the hope of Israel.

In view of the decision of the Assembly on Friday to omit any reference to the hope of Israel in its Statement on the Main Theme, we feel it our duty to offer an explanation of our convictions in the hope that it will help towards closer understanding with those from whom we differed.

Our concern in this issue is wholly biblical and is not to be confused with any political attitude towards the State of Israel.

We believe that Jesus Christ is the Saviour of all mankind. In Him there is neither Jew nor Greek, but we also believe that God elected Israel for the carrying out of His saving purpose. Jesus Christ as Man was a Jew. The Church of Jesus Christ is built upon the foundation of the Apostles and Prophets, all of whom were Jews, so that to be a member of the Christian Church is to be involved with the Jews in our one indivisible hope in Jesus Christ. Jesus, the Messiah of Israel, was accepted by Gentiles but rejected by His own people. Nevertheless God is so gracious and mighty that He even makes the crucifixion of His Son to be the salvation of the Gentiles (Rom. 11:11). Whether we are scandalized or not, that means that we are grafted into the old tree of Israel (Rom. 11:24), so that the people of the New Covenant cannot be separated from the people of the Old Covenant.

The New Testament, however, speaks also of the "fullness" of Israel, when God will manifest His glory by bringing back His "eldest son" into the one fold of His grace (Rom. 11:12-36; Matt. 23:29). This belief is an indispensable element of our one united hope for Jew and Gentile in Jesus Christ. Our hope in Christ's coming victory includes our hope for Israel in Christ, in His victory over the blindness of His own people. To expect Jesus Christ means to hope for the conversion of the Jewish people, and to love Him means to love the people of God's promise.

In view of the grievous guilt of Christian people towards the Jews throughout the history of the Church, we are certain that:

> the Church cannot rest until the title of Christ to the Kingdom is recognized by His own people according to the flesh. [1]

We cannot be one in Christ nor can we truly believe and witness to the promise of God if we do not recognize that it is still valid for the people of the promise made to Abraham. Therefore we invite all men to join with us in praising and magnifying that God who "concluded them all in unbelief that He might have mercy upon all" (Rom. 11:32).

Signed

H. Berkhof, *Holland*

M. Boegner, *France*

A. Koechlin, *Switzerland*

P. Maury, *France*

T.F. Torrance, *Scotland*

H. Vogel, *Germany*

J. Sittler, *USA*

O.S. Tomkins, *England*

J. Smemo, *Norway*

E. Schlink, *Germany*

H.I. Yochum, *USA*

N.A. Winter, *USA*

H. d'Espine, *Switzerland*

R.S. Louden, *Scotland*

H.F. Schuh, *USA*

A.E. Haefner, *USA*

J. Hromadka, *Czechoslovakia*

D.G. May, *Austria*

J.P. Van Heest, *Holland*

M. Niemöller, *Germany*

A.H. Ewald, *USA*

I. Pap, *Hungary*

S.B. Coles, *Canada*

G. Stratenwerth, *Germany*

---

[1] Findings of the Pre-Evanston Conference of the American Committee on the Christian Approach to the Jews, at Lake Geneva, 8-11 August 1954.

● From: *The Evanston Report: the Second Assembly of the World Council of Churches 1954*, London, SCM, 1955, pp.327f.

Document 3

The Third Assembly
of the World Council of Churches

*Reacting to fresh incidents of antisemitism in Germany and elsewhere
the Assembly, held from 19 November to 5 December 1961 in New Delhi,
passed a resolution on antisemitism.*

Upon recommendation to the Policy Reference Committee, and after
amendment from the floor, it was voted to adopt the following resolution:
The Third Assembly recalls the following words which were addressed to
the churches by the First Assembly of the World Council of Churches in 1948:

> We call upon all the churches we represent to denounce anti-semitism, no
> matter what its origin, as absolutely irreconcilable with the profession and
> practice of the Christian faith. Anti-semitism is sin against God and man. Only
> as we give convincing evidence to our Jewish neighbours that we seek for
> them the common rights and dignities which God wills for his children, can
> we come to such a meeting with them as would make it possible to share with
> them the best which God has given us in Christ.

The Assembly renews this plea in view of the fact that situations continue
to exist in which Jews are subject to discrimination and even persecution.
The Assembly urges its member churches to do all in their power to resist
every form of anti-semitism. In Christian teaching the historic events which
led to the Crucifixion should not be so presented as to fasten upon the Jewish
people of today responsibilities which belong to our corporate humanity and
not to one race or community. Jews were the first to accept Jesus and Jews are
not the only ones who do not yet recognize him.

● From: *The New Delhi Report. The Third Assembly of the World Council of
Churches 1961*, New York, Association Press, 1962, p. 148.

Document 4

The Commission
on Faith and Order

At its meeting held at Bristol from 29 July to 9 August 1967, the Commission on Faith and Order accepted the report of the Committee on the Church and the Jewish People and commended it for further theological study.

4. The Church and the Jewish People
Section I of the Fourth World Conference on Faith and Order at Montreal strongly commended for careful study the place of the people of Israel in relation to God's purpose in the Old and New Covenant, and that this subject should be referred to a commission. [1] *The Faith and Order Commission at Aarhus responded to this recommendation.* [2] *The study was carried out jointly by Faith and Order and the World Council of Churches' Committee on the Church and the Jewish People. An initial report drafted by a consultation in 1964 was circulated to many groups and individuals asking for their reactions and comments. Further revisions in the light of their responses lead to the following report.*

I. Introduction
There is a growing awareness in many churches today that an encounter with the Jews is essential. On various occasions in the past the World Council of Churches has condemned any form of anti-semitism. It is, however, necessary to think through the theological implications and the

---

[1] *The Fourth World Conference on Faith and Order,* eds P. C. Rodger and L. Vischer, Faith and Order Paper No. 42, London, SCM Press, 1964, para. 17, p.44.
[2] Aarhus Minutes, Faith and Order Paper No. 44, Geneva, WCC, 1965, p.42.

complex questions bound up with the Church's relation to the Jewish people in a more explicit and systematic way. This was, for instance, urged in the report of Section I on "The Church in the Purpose of God" at the Fourth World Conference on Faith and Order in Montreal in 1963. We hope that what follows here may be a contribution to such a study. We cannot pretend to offer more than that. We are aware of the shortcomings of this statement, and particularly that differences of opinion among us, which we have not yet been able to resolve, impose limits on what we can say. However, what we offer is, notwithstanding its limitations, new in the history of the World Council. We hope that this statement will stimulate a continuing discussion and will pave the way for a deeper common understanding and eventually a common declaration.

Both in biblical and contemporary language the words "Israel" and "Jews" can have various meanings. To avoid misunderstanding, in this document we have used the term "Israel" only when referring to the people in Old and New Testament times; no present-day political reference is intended or implied. When we speak about the people in post-biblical times we prefer to use the terms "Jews" or "Jewish people", the latter being a collective term designating the Jews all over the world. We find it hard to define in precise terms what it is that makes a Jew a Jew, though we recognize that both ethnic elements and religious traditions play a role.

In drawing up this document we set out to answer two distinct questions which were put to us: (1) in what way does the continuing existence of the Jews have theological significance for the Church, and (2) in what way should Christians give witness of their faith to Jews. The structure of this paper is to a great extent conditioned by this starting-point. It should also be kept in mind that we speak as Christian theologians; we are conscious of the fact that theological statements often have political, sociological or economic implications, even if that is not intended. That consideration, however, cannot be a reason for silence; we merely ask that this paper may be judged on its theological merits.

In our discussions we constantly kept the biblical writings in mind and tried to understand our questions in the light of the Scriptures. We realized that the evidence of the Bible, both Old and New Testaments, is varied and complex, and that we are all in constant danger of arbitrarily excluding parts of it. In re-thinking the place of the Jews in the history of salvation we should recognize that the question of Israel is very important in parts of the Gospels and the Pauline letters, but it seems to be less in evidence in other parts of the New Testament literature, though it is perhaps rarely entirely absent. The problems of interpreting the biblical evidence in regard to this question are just as difficult as they are in regard to other significant theological issues. Being aware of the danger of building one's thinking upon particular proof-texts, we have refrained from pointing to specific verses. We have tried, however, to be faithful to the overall meaning of the Bible and trust that the scriptural basis of what we say will be evident.

II. Historical considerations

The first community of Christians were Jews who had accepted Jesus as the Christ. They continued to belong to the Jewish communities and the relationship between them and their fellow-Jews was close, notwithstanding the tension that existed between them — a tension caused by the fact that the Christian Jews believed that the fullness of time had come in Christ and in the outpouring of the Spirit and that they therefore came to know themselves to be found in one fellowship with Gentiles who also believed in God through Jesus Christ. The two groups of Jews broke apart as the consequence of various facts: for example, the attitude of Christians towards the Law, the persecution of the Stephen group by Jews, the withdrawal from Jerusalem of the Christians during the great uprising 66-73 A.D., the increasing hostility between Jews and Christians which found expression in their respective liturgies, and in other ways. In the same period Christians of Gentile origin came greatly to outnumber the Jewish Christians. From this time on the history of Jews and Christians is one of ever increasing mutual estrangement. After Christianity became the accepted religion of the Roman state, the Jews were discriminated against and often even persecuted by the "Christian" state more often than not with ecclesiastical support. As a consequence, the so-called "dialogues" between Christian and Jewish theologians which were organized from time to time were never held on a footing of equality; the Jewish partners were not taken seriously.

In the past the existence of Jews outside the church and their refusal to accept the Christian faith prompted little serious theological questioning in official church circles. Christians generally thought about these questions in very stereotyped ways: the Jews as the Israel of the Old Testament had formerly been God's elect people, but this election had been transferred to the Church after Christ; the continuing existence of the Jews was primarily thought of in terms of divine rejection and retribution, because they were regarded as those who had killed Christ and whose hearts were so hardened that they continued to reject him.

Despite all this the separation between the Church and the Jewish people has never been absolute. In the liturgy of the church many Jewish elements have been preserved. And when in the middle of the second century Marcion tried to cut all ties by rejecting the Old Testament as God's revelation and by clearing the New Testament as far as possible of all its Old Testament concepts and references, the Church, by holding fast to the Old Testament, testified to the continuity between the old and the new covenants. She thereby in fact testified also to the common root and origin of the Church and the Jewish people, although this was not clearly realized; and only few Christians have been aware that this common root meant some kind of special relationship.

At the scholarly and theological level also there has always been contact between the two groups. In the Middle Ages especially, Christian theology and exegesis were strongly influenced by Jews, who for instance transmitted Aristotelian philosophy to them; the influence of Jewish mysticism upon Christian mystics, moreover, has been much stronger than is generally known. In the 16th century among Christians of the Western world a new awareness of their relationship with Jews arose, partly under the influence of humanism with its emphasis on the original biblical languages, partly because of the Reformation. Protestant attitudes were, however, by no means always positive. In pietism a strong love and hope for the Jewish people awoke, which in the 18th and 19th century found expression in the many attempts to come into missionary contact with Jews. But even so, there was little change in the thinking by Christians generally about the Jews. The time of the Enlightenment, with its common move towards toleration, brought improvement in the position of the Jews, at least in Western Europe. This happened in a cultural atmosphere in which there was a tendency to deny the particularity of the Jewish people. Outright anti-semitism, with its excesses and pogroms, seemed a thing of the past, although in most countries religions and social discrimination remained, the more insidious because it was often not fully conscious.

It is only since the beginning of this century, and even more especially since the last war, that churches, and not merely various individual Christians, have begun to rethink more systematically the nature of their relationship to the Jews. The main theological reason for this is probably the greater emphasis on biblical theology and the increased interest which the Old Testament in particular has received. It is self-evident that this emphasis was to a great extent caused by the preceding outbreak of anti-semitism in Germany and its rationalization on so-called Christian, ideological grounds. In the realm of biblical scholarship there is today increasing cooperation among Christians and Jews; many Christian theologians are aware of what they have learned from men like Rosenzweig, Buber and other Jewish scholars. The question of what is meant by election and the irrevocability of God's love is being asked again in a new way. The biblically important concept of "covenant" has become more central, and the relationship between the "old" and the "new" covenant is being restudied. In addition, Paul's wrestling with the baffling question of the disobedience of the greater part of his fellow-Jews has come up for consideration.

Besides these theological grounds, two historical events in the last thirty years have caused churches to direct their thinking more than before to their relationship to the Jewish people. In Europe persecution has taken place, greater and more brutal than could have been thought possible in our time, in which some six million Jews were annihilated in the most terrible way, not because of their personal actions or beliefs, but because of the mere fact that they had Jewish grandparents. The churches came to ask themselves whether this was simply the consequence of natural human wickedness or whether it had also another, theological dimension.

The second event was the creation of the State of Israel. This is of tremendous importance for the great majority of Jews; it has meant for them a new feeling of self-assurance and security. But this same event has also brought suffering and injustice to Arab people. We find it impossible to give a unanimous evaluation of its formation and of all the events connected with it, and therefore in this study do not make further mention of it. We realize, however, especially in view of the changed situation in the Middle East as a result of the war of June 1967, that also the question of the present state of Israel, and of its theological significance, if any, has to be taken up.

III. Theological considerations

We believe that God formed the people of Israel. There are certainly many factors of common history, ethnic background and religion, which can explain its coming into existence, but according to Old Testament faith as a whole, it was God's own will and decision which made this one distinct people with its special place in history. God is the God of the whole earth and of all nations, but he chose this particular people to be the bearer of a particular promise and to act as his covenant-partner and special instrument. He made himself known specifically to Israel, and showed this people what his will is for men on earth. Bound to him in love and obedience, it was called to live as God wants his people to live. In this way it was to become, as it were, a living revelation to others, in order that they also might come to know, trust, love and obey God. In dealing with Israel, God had in view the other nations; this was the road by which he came to them. In order words, in his love for Israel his love for mankind was manifested; in its election, Israel, without losing its own particularity, represented the others.

In the Old Testament Israel is shown to be an imperfect instrument; again and again it was untrue to its calling so that it often obscured rather than manifested God's will on earth. But even in its disobedience it was a witness to God, a witness to his judgment, which however terrible was seen as a form of his grace, for in punishment God was seeking to purify his people and to bring them back to himself; a witness also to his faithfulness and love, which did not let his people go, even when they turned away from him.

We believe that in Jesus Christ God's revelation in the Old Testament finds its fulfilment. Through him we see into the very heart of God, in him we see what it really means to say that God is the God of the covenant and loves man to the very end. As be became the man who was the perfect instrument of God's purpose, he took upon himself the vocation of his people. He, as its representative, fulfills Israel's task of obedience. In his resurrection it has become manifest that God's love is stronger than human sin. In him God has forgiven and wiped out sin and in him created his true covenant-partner.

A part of Israel recognized in Jesus as the Christ the full revelation of God. They believed that in him God himself was present, and that in his death and resurrection God acted decisively for the salvation of the world. Numerically they were perhaps only a very small minority, yet in these "few" God's purpose for the whole of Israel is manifested and confirmed. And together with Israel the Gentiles too were now called to the love and service of God. It cannot be otherwise; for if in Jesus Christ the fullness of time has really come, then the nations also must participate in God's salvation, and the separation of Israel is abolished. This is what the church is: Israel having come to recognize God in Christ, together with the Gentiles who are engrafted into Israel, so that now Jew and Gentile become one in Christ. It is only in this way that the Church is the continuation of the Israel of the Old Testament, God's chosen people, called upon to testify to his mighty acts for men, and to be his fellow-workers in this world.

Christ himself is the ground and substance of this continuity. This is underlined by the preservation of the Old Testament in the Church as an integral part of her worship and tradition. The existence of Christians of Jewish descent provides a visible manifestation of that same continuity, though many Christians are hardly aware of this. The presence of such members in a Church which in the course of time has become composed predominantly of Gentiles, witnesses to the trustworthiness of God's promises, and should serve to remind the Church of her origin in Israel. We are not advocating separate congregations for them. History has shown the twofold danger which lies in this: the danger of discriminating despite all intention to the contrary, and the danger that such separate congregations tend to evolve sectarian traits. But more important than these considerations is that in Christ the dividing wall has been broken down and Jew and Gentile are to form one new man; thus any separation in the church has been made impossible.

However, without detracting in any way from what has just been said, we should remember that there is room for all kinds of people and cultures in the church. This implies that Jews who become Christians are not simply required to abandon their Jewish traditions and ways of thinking; in certain circumstances it may therefore be right to form special groups which are composed mainly of Jewish Christians.

The fact that by far the greater part of Israel did not recognize God in Jesus Christ posed a burning question for Paul, not primarily because of the crucifixion, but because even after Christ's resurrection they still rejected him. The existence of Jews today who do not accept him puts the same question to us, because in this respect the situation today is basically the same as it was in Paul's time.

We are convinced that the Jewish people still have a significance of their own for the Church. It is not merely that by God's grace they have preserved in their faith truths and insights into his revelation which we have tended to forget; .... But also it seems to us that by their very existence in spite of all attempt to destroy them, they make it manifest that God has not abandoned them. In this way they are a living and visible sign of God's faithfulness to men, an indication that he also upholds those who do not find it possible to recognize him in his Son. While we see their continuing existence as pointing to God's love and mercy, we explicitly reject any thought of considering their suffering during the ages as a proof of any special guilt. Why, in God's purpose, they have suffered in that way, we as outsiders do not know. What we do know, however, is the guilt of Christians who have all too often stood on the side of the persecutors instead of the persecuted.

Conscious of this guilt we find it impossible to speak in a generalizing way of Christian obedience over against Jewish disobedience. It is true that we believe that Jesus Christ is the truth and the way for every man, and that for everyone faith in him is salvation. But we also know that it is only by grace that we have come to accept him and that even in our acceptance we are still in many ways disobedient. We have therefore no reason to pride ourselves over against others. For Christians as well as Jews can live only by the forgiveness of sin, and by God's mercy.

We believe that in the future also God in faithfulness will not abandon the Jewish people, but that his promise and calling will ultimately prevail so as to bring them to their salvation. This is to us an assurance that we are allowed to hope for the salvation of all who do not yet recognize Christ. So long as the Jews do not worship with the Church the one God and Father of Jesus Christ, they are to us a perpetual reminder that God's purpose and promise are not yet realized in their fullness, that we have still much to hope for the world, looking for the time when the Kingdom of God will become plainly and gloriously manifest.

All this we can say together. However, this considerable agreement, for which we are grateful indeed, should not conceal the fact that when the question is raised of the theological identity of Israel with the Jewish people of today we find ourselves divided. This division is due not only to the differences in the interpretation of the biblical evidence, but also in the weight which is given to various passages. We might characterize our differences, rather schematically, as follows:

Some are convinced that, despite the elements of continuity that admittedly exist between present-day Jews and Israel, to speak of the continued election of the Jewish people alongside the Church is inadmissible. It is the Church alone, they say, that is, theologically speaking, the continuation of Israel as the people of God, to which now all nations belong. Election and vocation are solely in Christ, and are to be grasped in faith. To speak otherwise is to deny that the one people of God, the Church, is the body of Christ which cannot be broken. In Christ it is made manifest that God's love and his promises apply to all men. The Christian hope for the Jews is the same as it is for all men: that they may come to the knowledge of the truth, Jesus Christ our Lord. This does not imply any denial of the distinctive and significant witness to Christ which the Jews still bear. For their continued separate existence is the direct result of the dual role which Israel as God's elect people has played: through them salvation has come to the world, and they represented at the crucial time of human history man's rejection of God's salvation offered in Christ.

Others of us are of the opinion that it is not enough merely to assert some kind of continuity between the present-day Jews — whether religious or not — and ancient Israel, but that they actually are still Israel, i.e. that they still are God's elect people. These would stress that after Christ the one people of God is broken asunder, one part being the Church which accepts Christ, the other part Israel outside the Church, which rejects him, but which even in this rejection remains in a special sense beloved by God. They see this election manifested specifically in the fact that the existence of the Jewish people in this world still reveals the truth that God's promises are irrevocable, that he will uphold the covenant of love which he has made with Israel. Further they see this continuing election in the fact that God has linked the final hope of the world to the salvation of the Jews, in the day when he will heal the broken body of his one people, Israel and the church.

These two views, described above, should however not be understood as posing a clear-cut alternative. Many hold positions somewhere in between, and without glossing over the real disagreements which exist, in some cases these positions can be so close, that they seem to rest more on different emphases than to constitute real contradictions. But even where our positions seem particularly irreconcilable, we cannot be content to let the matter rest as it is. For the conversation among us has only just begun and we realize that in this question the entire self-understanding of the Church is at stake.

IV. The Church and her witness

In the foregoing it is set forth that the Church stands in a unique relationship to the Jews. Every one who accepts Christ and becomes a member of his Church shares thereby in this special relation, being brought face to face with the Jewish people. That is to say that the problem we are dealing with in this paper is not one which confronts only the so-called Western churches, but concerns every Christian of whatever race, cultural or religious background he may be. So too the Old Testament is not only of importance for those whose culture is to a greater or lesser degree rooted in it, but becomes also the spiritual heritage of those Christians whose own ethnic culture is not touched by it.

The existence of this unique relationship raises the question as to whether it conditions the way in which Christians have to bear witness of Jesus to Jews.

We all agree that the Church is the special instrument of God, which is called to testify in her word and her life to his love revealed in its fullness in his Son. She has to proclaim that in Christ's cross and resurrection it has become manifest that God's love and mercy embrace all men. Moreover, being rooted in his reconciliation, she is called to cross all frontiers of race, culture and nationality, and all other barriers which separate man from man. Therefore we are convinced that no one can be excluded from her message of forgiveness and reconciliation; to do otherwise would be disobedience to the Lord of the church and a denial of her very nature, a negation of her fundamental openness and catholicity.

In the World Council of Churches much thinking has been done about the question of how the Church can give her witness in such a way that she respects the beliefs and convictions of those who do not share her faith in Christ, and perhaps, with God's help, bring them in full freedom to accept it. It is agreed that in an encounter with non-Christian people real openness is demanded, a willingness to listen to what the other has to say, and a readiness to be questioned by him and learn from his insights. This means that at all times Christians have to guard against an arrogant or paternalistic attitude. Moreover, the way in which they approach different men in different circumstances cannot be a single one; they should do their utmost to gain a real understanding of the life and thinking of the non-Christian, for only thereby can they speak to his situation in their witness.

That this is the generally accepted attitude for Christians to men of other faiths can be seen from the statement on "Christian Witness, Proselytism and Religious Liberty" accepted at the Third Assembly of the World Council of Churches in New Delhi, 1961, and from the declaration of the Commission on World Mission and Evangelism at Mexico City, 1963. It will therefore be evident that we consider the alternatives of mission or dialogue, which formerly was perhaps justified, untenable today. We are convinced that an encounter with non-Christians on the lines indicated above can be a real enrichment for the church in which she not only gives but also receives.

The very fact that the particular situation in which the Christian witness is given must always be taken into account, applies of course also to the Jews. Moreover, where they are concerned this consideration receives a special dimension, for with no other people does the Church have such close ties. Christians and Jews are rooted in the same divine history of salvation, as has already been shown; both claim to be heirs of the same Old Testament. Christian and Jewish faiths share also a common hope that the world and its history are being led by God to the full realization and manifestation of his kingdom.

However, in an encounter between Christians and Jews not only the common ties are to be considered but also their age-long alienation and the terrible guilt of discrimination which Christians share with the world, and which in our own time has culminated in the gas-chamber and the destruction of a large part of European Jewry. Though certainly not all Christians are equally guilty and though anti-semitism has played no particular role in the Oriental and in the so-called younger churches, we all have to realize that Christian words have now become disqualified and suspect in the ears of most Jews. Therefore often the best, and sometimes perhaps even the only way in which Christians today can testify to the Jewish people about their faith in Christ may be not so much in explicit words but by service.

We all are thus basically of one mind about the actual form which in practice the Christian encounter with the Jewish people has to take. We differ, however, among ourselves when we try to analyze and to formulate this common attitude in theological terms. The differences which exist in this respect are closely connected with the ones we noted before. There it was remarked that the very self-understanding of the Church was at stake (par. 22). Here, even more, our differences are bound up with differences in ecclesiology, or rather with the different ecclesiological points on which we lay stress. If the main emphasis is put on the concept of the Church as the body of Christ, the Jewish people are seen as being outside. The Christian attitude to them is considered to be in principle the same as to men of other faiths and the mission of the Church is to bring them, either individually or corporately, to the acceptance of Christ, so that they become members of his body. Those who hold this view would generally want to stress that besides service to the Jews it is also legitimate and even necessary to witness in a more explicit way as well, be it through individuals, or special societies, or churches.

If, on the other hand, the Church is primarily seen as the people of God, it is possible to regard the Church and the Jewish people together as forming the one people of God, separated from one another for the time being, yet with the promise that they will ultimately become one. Those who follow this line of thinking would say that the Church should consider her attitude towards the Jews theologically and in principle as being different from the attitude she has to all other men who do not belive in Christ. It should be thought of more in terms of ecumenical engagement in order to heal the breach than of missionary witness in which she hopes for conversion.

Again it should be pointed out that these views are not static positions; there are gradual transitions between the two and often it is more a question of a more-or-less than of an either-or. That is in the nature of the matter. For the Church must be thought of both as the body of Christ and as the people of God, and these two concepts express the one reality from different angles.

But even though we have not yet reached a common theological evaluation of the Christian encounter with Jews, we all emphatically reject any form of "proselytizing", in the derogatory sense which the word has come to carry in our time, where it is used for the corruption of witness in cajolery, undue pressure or intimidation, or other improper methods (see the New Delhi declaration on "Christian Witness, Proselytism and Religious Liberty").

V. Ecumenical relevance

We are convinced that the Church's rethinking of her theology with regard to the question of Israel and her conversation with the Jewish people can be of real importance to the ecumenical movement. In this way questions are posed which touch the foundation and the heart of Christian faith. Though these questions are also being asked for other reasons, it is our experience that here they are being put in a particularly penetrating form. Because there is no doctrine of Christian theology which is not touched and influenced in some way by this confrontation with the Jewish people, it is impossible for us here to develop fully its implications. We can only indicate some salient points.

1. The documents of the Old Testament belong to the heritage which the churches have received from and have in common with the Jews. In a theological encounter of the two groups the question of the right understanding of these writings will necessarily come to the fore, the Jews placing them in the context of the Talmud and Midrash, the churches in that of the New Testament. Thereby Christians are called upon to analyze the criteria they use in their interpretation of the Bible. Clarity in this respect will help the churches in their search together for the biblical truth.

2. The Old Testament is also part of the common heritage that lies beyond the separation of the churches themselves. Differences in its evaluation and interpretation may result in different understandings of the New Testament. When in their meeting with Jewish theologians

the churches are driven to reconsider whether they have understood the Old Testament aright, and perhaps coming to new insights into it, it may well help them also to understand the Gospel in a deeper and fuller way and so overcome one-sided and different conceptions which keep them apart.

3. Jewish faith regards itself as being based on God's revelation written down in the Bible as it is interpreted and actualized in the ongoing tradition of the Jewish believing community. Therefore, in their theological dialogue with Jews the churches will be confronted with the question of tradition and Scripture. When this problem, which has been a cause of dissension between Christians for a long time, is considered in this new setting, the churches may gain insights which can contribute to a greater understanding and agreement among themselves.

4. The emphasis made by Jews in their dialogue with Christians on justice and righteousness in this world reminds the churches of the divine promise of a new earth and warns them not to express their eschatological hope onesidedly in other-worldly terms.

   Equally, reflection in the light of the Bible on the Jewish concept of man as God's covenant-partner working for the sanctification of the world and for the bringing in of the kingdom should prompt the churches to reconsider their old controversy over the cooperation of man in salvation.

5. The existence of Jews, both those who have become Christians and those who have not, compels the churches to clarify their own belief about election. They must ask themselves whether election is not a constitutive element in God's action with men, whether it does not have an unshakable objectivity which precedes the response of those who are elected, but which on the other hand requires ever anew acceptance by faith, realized in human acts of obedience. A study of these questions may bring closer together those who stress the prevenient grace of God and those who put the main accent on the human decision of faith.

VI. Some implications

Finally we want to point to some implications of this study. Needless to say, they can be indicated only briefly; we hope that in the future some of these points will be taken up and further elaborated and acted upon. In this connection we recall the following words of the Third Assembly in New Delhi, which renewed the plea against anti-semitism of the First

Assembly in 1948, adding that "the Assembly urges its member churches to do all in their power to resist every form of anti-semitism. In Christian teaching the historic events which led to the Crucifixion should not be so presented as to fasten upon the Jewish people of today responsibilities which belong to our corporate humanity and not to one race or community. Jews were the first to accept Jesus and Jews are not the only ones who do not yet recognize him."

The last sentences of the statement just quoted refer to the question of the responsibility of the Jews today for the crucifixion. This question has both a historical and a theological dimension. (1) Modern scholarship has generally come to the conclusion that it is historically wrong to hold the Jewish people of Jesus' time responsible as a whole for his death. Only a small minority of those who were in Jerusalem were actively hostile to him, and even these were only indirectly instrumental in bringing about his death: the actual sentence was imposed by the Roman authorities. Moreover, it is impossible to hold the Jews today responsible for what a few of their forefathers may have participated in nearly twenty centuries ago. (2) Theologically speaking we believe that this small minority, acting together with the Roman authorities, expressed the sin and blindness common to all mankind. Those passages in the New Testament which charge the Jews with the crucifixion of Jesus must be read within the wider biblical understanding of Israel as representative of all men. In their rejection of Christ our own rejection of him is mirrored.

We recommend that, especially in religious instruction and preaching, great care be taken not to picture the Jews in such a way as to foster inadvertently a kind of "Christian" anti-semitism. In addition to the way in which the crucifixion is often taught, we have in mind, among other things, the historically mistaken image often given to the Pharisees, the misconception of the Law of the Old Testament and its so-called legalism, and the stress repeatedly placed upon the disobedience of the Jews according to the Old and New Testaments, without it being made sufficiently clear that those who denounced this disobedience were also Jews, one with their people notwithstanding their denunciation.

Similarly, some Christian prayers contain expressions which, whatever their meaning formerly was, can easily promote misunderstanding today. We feel that it would help if the churches would re-examine both traditional liturgies and also lessons, hymns and other texts used in worship from the point of view set out in this document.

The fact that the Jewish people is of continued significance for the Church should also have its effect on the way history is presented.

Because of this special relationship all through the ages, church history cannot rightly be taught without taking into account its impact on the history of the Jews, and vice versa. We are of the opinion that theological teaching and text books are in general inadequate in this respect and need to be reconsidered and supplemented.

There is a general tendency among Christians to equate the faith of the Old Testament with Jewish religion today. This is an over-simplification which does not do justice to Jewish understanding of the Old Testament and to subsequent developments. Here the oral law must be specially mentioned, for it has played such a central role in shaping Jewish life and thought, and still continues to be of paramount importance for large groups.

We should also be aware that many, while affirming that they belong to the Jewish people, do not call themselves believing Jews. For a real encounter with the Jews we consider it imperative to have knowledge and genuine understanding of their thinking and their problems both in the secular and in the religious realm. We should always remain aware that we are dealing with actual, living people in all their variety, and not with an abstract concept of our own.

* * *

We have often been aware in our discussions that no problem should be examined in isolation. Nor should this one be, since there may be a danger that, instead of reducing anti-semitism, we may even increase it by concentrating on this issue.

Through our study together it has been brought home to us that much thinking still has to be done, and how impossible it is to ignore or avoid the theological questions in this area. We feel assured that an ongoing encounter with Jews can mean a real enrichment of our faith. Christians should therefore be alert to every such possibility, both in the field of social cooperation and especially on the deeper level of theological discussion. We realize that at the moment many Jews are not willing to be involved with Christians in a common dialogue; in that case Christians must respect this expressed or silent wish and not force themselves upon them. But when such conversation is possible, it should be held in a spirit of mutual respect and openness, searching together and questioning one another, trusting that we together with the Jews will grow into a deeper understanding of the revelation of the God of Abraham, Isaac and Jacob.

What form this further understanding may take, we must be willing to leave in his hands, confident that he will lead both Jews and Christians into the fullness of his truth.

The Commission accepted this report and commended it for further theological study on a wider geographical scale. It was, however, felt that such issues as: (1) the concepts of salvation and election, and (2) the nature of God in relation to the two concepts of the People of God and the Body of Christ require a more thorough study and a more detailed examination.

● From: *New Directions in Faith and Order, Bristol 1967,* Faith and Order Paper No. 50, Geneva, WCC, 1968.

Document 5

The Fourth Assembly of the World Council of Churches

The Assembly, held at Uppsala from 4 to 20 July 1968, one year after the Six-Day War, passed a "Statement on the Middle East".

1. We are deeply concerned that the menace of the situation in the Middle East shows no present sign of abating. The resolutions of the United Nations have not been implemented, the territorial integrity of the nations involved is not respected, occupation continues. No settlement is in sight and a new armament race is being mounted.

In these circumstances we reaffirm the statement of the Heraklion Central Committee in August 1967, and make the following points based upon it:

a) The independence and territorial integrity and security of all nations in the area must be guaranteed. Annexation by force must not be condoned.

b) The World Council of Churches must continue to join with all who search for a solution of the refugee and displaced person problems.

c) Full religious freedom and access to holy places must continue to be guaranteed to the communities of all three historic religions preferably by international agreement.

d) National armaments should be limited to the lowest level consistent with national security.

e) The great world powers must refrain from pursuing their own exclusive interests in the area.

2. The forthcoming report of the Special Representative of the United Nations Secretary General is urgently awaited, and the Assembly earnestly hopes that it may open the way to a settlement.

3. It is the special responsibility of the World Council of Churches and of its member churches to discern ways in which religious factors affect the conflict.

● From: *The Uppsala Report 1968*, ed. Norman Goodall, Geneva, WCC, 1968, p.189.

Document 6

The Fifth Assembly
of the World Council of Churches

The Assembly, held at Nairobi from 23 November to 10 December 1975, adopted two statements: "The Middle East" and "Jerusalem".

The Middle East

1. The World Council of Churches has expressed concern regarding the situation in the Middle East on previous occasions. Events which have occurred in the area during the meeting of the Fifth Assembly in Nairobi have demonstrated anew that tensions persist there unabated.

2. We are concerned at the continued escalation of military power in the area which can only aggravate the threat to world peace from the unresolved conflict; and stress the necessity for the great world powers to cease furnishing the arms which maintain and aggravate the tensions.

3. We recognize that an international consensus has emerged as the basis for peaceful settlement on the following:
a) Withdrawal by Israel from territories occupied in 1967.
b) The right of all states including Israel and the Arab states to live in peace within secure and recognized boundaries.
c) The implementation of the rights of the Palestinian people to self-determination.
We are encouraged that the parties to the conflict seem to be progressively willing to accept these principles.

4. We recognize the Second Sinai Disengagement Agreement as a means of reducing tension between Egypt and Israel. However, since it is not addressed to the fears and distrust among Israel, other neighbouring states, and the Palestinian people, this Agreement must be followed soon by resumption of the Geneva Peace Conference for reaching a total

settlement on the basis of the principles mentioned above. The Geneva Conference should necessarily involve all parties concerned, including the Palestinians.

5. We note that some Arab states have recently declared their readiness, with the participation of the Palestine Liberation Organization, to seek agreement with Israel based upon these principles.

6. Although the parties have not trusted one another sufficiently until now to engage in dialogue, full mutual recognition by the parties must be seen not as a precondition to, but rather as a product of, the negotiation. We call upon all parties to take those steps essential to negotiations with hope for success. Among these steps, we emphasize the cessation of all military activity, both regular and irregular, including terrorism.

7. Peace in the Middle East must be based upon justice and security for all concerned. The wellbeing of each party depends upon the wellbeing of all other parties. We urge the churches to help their constituencies to have more accurate information on and more sensitive awareness of the various discussions of the Middle East conflict. The churches could thus help to promote natural trust among the parties and to develop a responsible involvement in peaceful solution on the part of their members and the government of their countries. This opportunity is open to churches within the area and the churches outside the area as well.

Jerusalem

1. For many millions of Christians throughout the world, as well as for the adherents of the two great sister monotheistic religions, namely Judaism and Islam, Jerusalem continues to be a focus of deepest religious inspiration and attachment. It is therefore their responsibility to cooperate in the creation of conditions that will ensure that Jerusalem is a city open to the adherents of all three religions, where they can meet and live together. The tendency to minimize Jerusalem's importance for any of these religions should be avoided.

2. The special legislation regulating the relationship of the Christian communities and the authorities, guaranteed by international treaties (Paris 1856 and Berlin 1878) and the League of Nations and known as the Status Quo of the Holy Places must be fully safeguarded and confirmed in any agreement concerning Jerusalem. Christian Holy Places in Jerusalem and neighbouring areas belong to the greatest extent to member churches of the WCC. On the basis of the Status Quo none of the church authorities of a given denomination could represent unilaterally and on behalf of all

Christians the Christian point of view, each church authority of a given denomination representing only its own point of view.

3. Many member churches of the WCC are deeply concerned about the Christian Holy Places. However, the question of Jerusalem is not only a matter of protection of the Holy Places, it is organically linked with living faiths and communities of people in the Holy City. Therefore the Assembly deems it essential that the Holy Shrines should not become mere monuments of visitation, but should serve as living places of worship integrated and responsive to Christian communities who continue to maintain their life and roots within the Holy City and for those who out of religious attachments want to visit them.

4. While recognizing the complexity and emotional implications of the issues surrounding the future status of Jerusalem, the Assembly believes that such status has to be determined within the general context of the settlement of the Middle East conflict in its totality.

5. However, the Assembly thinks that apart from any politics, the whole settlement of the inter-religious problem of the Holy Places should take place under an international aegis and guarantee which ought to be respected by the parties concerned as well as the ruling authorities.

6. The Assembly recommends that the above should be worked out with the most directly concerned member churches, as well as with the Roman Catholic Church. These issues should also become subjects for dialogue with Jewish and Muslim counterparts.

7. The Assembly expresses its profound hope and fervent prayers for the peace and welfare of the Holy City and all its inhabitants.

• From: *Breaking Barriers*, the official report of the Fifth Assembly of the World Council of Churches, Nairobi, 23 November-10 December 1975, London, SPCK, and Grand Rapids, Wm B. Eerdmans, 1976, pp.162-165.

Document 7

The Executive Committee
of the World Council of Churches

As the result of a long process of discussion within the WCC and its member churches the document on "Ecumenical Considerations on Jewish-Christian Dialogue" had been "received and commended to the churches for study and action" by the Executive Committee of the WCC at Geneva on 16 July 1982.

Ecumenical Considerations
on Jewish-Christian Dialogue

Historical note

In 1975 the Consultation on the Church and the Jewish People (CCJP) voted to begin the process that has borne fruit in these Ecumenical Considerations on Jewish-Christian Dialogue. The first step was to request preparatory papers from the various regions with experience in Jewish-Christian dialogue. When the Central Committee adopted "Guidelines on Dialogue" in 1979, work on developing specific suggestions for Jewish-Christian dialogue began and, after a period of drafting and revisions, a draft was presented for comments to the International Jewish Committee on Interreligious Consultations (IJCIC), the CCJP's primary Jewish dialogue partner. After discussion in the DFI Working Group in 1980, a revised draft was circulated among interested persons in the churches and comments solicited. Many and substantial comments and suggestions were received.

When it met in London Colney, England, in June 1981, the CCJP adopted its final revisions and submitted them to the DFI Working Group, which adopted them at its meeting in Bali, Indonesia, 2 January 1982, having made its own revisions at a few points. On the advice of the February 1982 WCC Executive Committee, various concerned member churches and various members of the CCJP were further consulted in order to revise and re-order the text. The result, "Ecumenical Considerations on Jewish-Christian Dialogue", was "received and commended to the churches for study and action" by the Executive Committee of the World Council of Churches at Geneva on 16 July 1982.

When it adopted "Guidelines on Dialogue" in 1979, the Central Committee commended them to the member churches "for their consideration and discussion, testing and evaluation, and for their elaboration in each specific situation". These "Ecumenical Considerations on Jewish-Christian Dialogue" constitute one such elaboration for dialogue with people of a particular faith. It is anticipated that other specific dialogues with Muslims, Buddhists, Hindus, Marxists, and others will in the future lead to the formulation of additional "ecumenical considerations" relative to dialogue with such adherents of particular faiths and ideologies. In every case, these "ecumenical considerations" should be understood as stages along the way, to be amplified and refined as deeper and wider dialogue provides greater and more sensitive insight into relationships among the diverse peoples of God's one world.

1. Preface

1.1: "One of the functions of dialogue is to allow participants to describe and witness to their faith in their own terms. This is of primary importance since self-serving descriptions of other peoples' faith are one of the roots of prejudice, stereotyping, and condescension. Listening carefully to the neighbours' self-understanding enables Christians better to obey the commandment not to bear false witness against their neighbours, whether those neighbours be of long-established religious, cultural or ideological traditions or members of new religious groups. It should be recognized by partners in dialogue that any religion or ideology claiming universality, apart from having an understanding of itself, will also have its own interpretations of other religions and ideologies as part of its own self-understanding. Dialogue gives an opportunity for a mutual questioning of the understanding partners have about themselves and others. It is out of a reciprocal willingness to listen and learn that significant dialogue grows." (WCC Guidelines on Dialogue, III.4)

1.2: In giving such guidelines applicable to all dialogues, the World Council of Churches speaks primarily to its member churches as it defines the need for and gifts to be received by dialogue. People of other faiths may choose to define their understanding of dialogue, and their expectations as to how dialogue with Christians may affect their own traditions and attitudes and may lead to a better understanding of Christianity. Fruitful "mutual questioning of the understanding partners have about themselves and others" requires the spirit of dialogue. But the WCC Guidelines do not predict what partners in dialogue may come to learn about themselves, their history, and their problems. Rather they speak within the churches about faith, attitudes, actions, and problems of Christians.

1.3: In all dialogues distinct asymmetry between any two communities of faith becomes an important fact. Already terms like faith, theology, religion, scripture, people, etc. are not innocent or neutral. Partners in dialogue may rightly question the very language in which each thinks about religious matters.

1.4: In the case of Jewish-Christian dialogue a specific historical and theological asymmetry is obvious. While an understanding of Judaism in New Testament times becomes an integral and indispensable part of any Christian theology, for Jews, a "theological" understanding of Christianity is of a less than essential or integral significance. Yet, neither community of faith has developed without awareness of the other.

1.5: The relations between Jews and Christians have unique characteristics because of the ways in which Christianity historically emerged out of Judaism. Christian understandings of that process constitute a necessary part of the dialogue and give urgency to the enterprise. As Christianity came to define its own identity over against Judaism, the church developed its own understandings, definitions and terms for what it had inherited from Jewish traditions, and for what it read in the Scriptures common to Jews and Christians. In the process of defining its own identity the church defined Judaism, and assigned to the Jews definite roles in its understanding of God's acts of salvation. It should not be surprising that Jews resent those Christian theologies in which they as a people are assigned to play a negative role. Tragically, such patterns of thought in Christianity have often led to overt acts of condescension, persecutions, and worse.

1.6: Bible-reading and worshipping Christians often believe that they "know Judaism" since they have the Old Testament, the records of Jesus' debates with Jewish teachers and the early Christian reflections on the

Judaism of their times. Furthermore, no other religious tradition has been so thoroughly "defined" by preachers and teachers in the church as has Judaism. This attitude is often enforced by lack of knowledge about the history of Jewish life and thought through the 1,900 years since the parting of the ways of Judaism and Christianity.

1.7: For these reasons there is special urgency for Christians to listen, through study and dialogue, to ways in which Jews understand their history and their traditions, their faith and their obedience "in their own terms". Furthermore, a mutual listening to how each is perceived by the other may be a step towards understanding the hurts, overcoming the fears, and correcting the misunderstandings that have thrived on isolation.

1.8: Both Judaism and Christianity comprise a wide spectrum of opinions, options, theologies, and styles of life and service. Since generalizations often produce stereotyping, Jewish-Christian dialogue becomes the more significant by aiming at as full as possible a representation of views within the two communities of faith.

2. Towards a Christian understanding of Jews and Judaism

2.1: Through dialogue with Jews many Christians have come to appreciate the richness and vitality of Jewish faith and life in the covenant and have been enriched in their own understandings of God and the divine will for all creatures.

2.2: In dialogue with Jews, Christians have learned that the actual history of Jewish faith and experiences does not match the images of Judaism that have dominated a long history of Christian teaching and writing, images that have been spread by Western culture and literature into other parts of the world.

2.3: A classical Christian tradition sees the church replacing Israel as God's people, and the destruction of the second temple of Jerusalem as a warrant for this claim. The covenant of God with the people of Israel was only a preparation for the coming of Christ, after which it was abrogated.

2.4: Such a theological perspective has had fateful consequences. As the church replaced the Jews as God's people, the Judaism that survived was seen as a fossilized religion of legalism — a view now perpetuated by scholarship which claims no theological interests. Judaism of the first centuries before and after the birth of Jesus was therefore called "Late Judaism". The Pharisees were considered to represent the acme of legalism, Jews and Jewish groups were portrayed as negative models, and the truth and beauty of Christianity were thought to be enhanced by setting up Judaism as false and ugly.

2.5: Through a renewed study of Judaism and in dialogue with Jews, Christians have become aware that Judaism in the time of Christ was in an early stage of its long life. Under the leadership of the Pharisees the Jewish people began a spiritual revival of remarkable power, which gave them the vitality capable of surviving the catastrophe of the loss of the temple. It gave birth to Rabbinic Judaism which produced the Mishnah and Talmud and built the structures for a strong and creative life through the centuries.

2.6: As a Jew, Jesus was born into this tradition. In that setting he was nurtured by the Hebrew Scriptures, which he accepted as authoritative and to which he gave a new interpretation in his life and teaching. In this context Jesus announced that the kingdom of God was at hand, and in his resurrection his followers found the confirmation of his being both Lord and Messiah.

2.7: Christians should remember that some of the controversies reported in the New Testament between Jesus and the "scribes and Pharisees" find parallels within Pharisaism itself and its heir, Rabbinic Judaism. These controversies took place in a Jewish context, but when the words of Jesus came to be used by Christians who did not identify with the Jewish people as Jesus did, such sayings often became weapons in anti-Jewish polemics and thereby their original intention was tragically distorted. An internal Christian debate is now taking place on the question of how to understand passages in the New Testament that seem to contain anti-Jewish references.

2.8: Judaism, with its rich history of spiritual life, produced the Talmud as the normative guide for Jewish life in thankful response to the grace of God's covenant with the people of Israel. Over the centuries important commentaries, profound philosophical works and poetry of spiritual depth have been added. For Judaism the Talmud is central and authoritative. Judaism is more than the religion of the Scriptures of Israel. What Christians call the Old Testament has received in the Talmud and later writings interpretations that for Jewish tradition share in the authority of Moses.

2.9: For Christians the Bible with the two Testaments is also followed by traditions of interpretation, from the Church Fathers to the present time. Both Jews and Christians live in the continuity of their Scripture and Tradition.

2.10: Christians as well as Jews look to the Hebrew Bible as the story recording Israel's sacred memory of God's election and covenant with this people. For Jews, it is their own story in historical continuity with the

present. Christians, mostly of gentile background since early in the life of
the church, believe themselves to be heirs to this same story by grace in
Jesus Christ. The relationship between the two communities, both worshipping the God of Abraham, Isaac and Jacob, is a given historical fact,
but how it is to be understood theologically is a matter of internal
discussion among Christians, a discussion that can be enriched by
dialogue with Jews.

2.11: Both commonalities and differences between the two faiths need
to be examined carefully. Finding in the Scriptures of the Old and New
Testaments the authority sufficient for salvation, the Christian Church
shares Israel's faith in the One God, whom it knows in the Spirit as the
God and Father of the Lord Jesus Christ. For Christians, Jesus Christ is
the only begotten Son of the Father, through whom millions have come to
share in the love of, and to adore, the God who first made covenant with
the people of Israel. Knowing the One God in Jesus Christ through the
Spirit, therefore, Christians worship that God with a Trinitarian confession to the One God, the God of Creation, Incarnation and Pentecost. In
so doing, the Church worships in a language foreign to Jewish worship
and sensitivities, yet full of meaning to Christians.

2.12: Christians and Jews both believe that God has created men and
women as the crown of creation and has called them to be holy and to
exercise stewardship over the creation in accountability to God. Jews and
Christians are taught by their Scriptures and traditions to know themselves responsible to their neighbours especially to those who are weak, poor
and oppressed. In various and distinct ways they look for the day in which
God will redeem the creation. In dialogue with Jews many Christians
come to a more profound appreciation of the Exodus hope of liberation,
and pray and work for the coming of righteousness and peace on earth.

2.13: Christians learn through dialogue with Jews that for Judaism the
survival of the Jewish people is inseparable from its obedience to God and
God's covenant.

2.14: During long periods, both before and after the emergence of
Christianity, Jews found ways of living in obedience to Torah, maintain-
ing and deepening their calling as a peculiar people in the midst of the
nations. Through history there are times and places in which Jews were
allowed to live, respected and accepted by the cultures in which they
resided, and where their own culture thrived and made a distinct and
sought-after contribution to their Christian and Muslim neighbours. Often
lands not dominated by Christians proved most favourable for Jewish
diaspora living. There were even times when Jewish thinkers came to

"make a virtue out of necessity" and considered diaspora living to be the distinct genius of Jewish existence.

2.15: Yet, there was no time in which the memory of the Land of Israel and of Zion, the city of Jerusalem, was not central in the worship and hope of the Jewish people. "Next year in Jerusalem" was always part of Jewish worship in the diaspora. And the continued presence of Jews in the Land and in Jerusalem was always more than just one place of residence among all the others.

2.16: Jews differ in their interpretations of the State of Israel, as to its religious and secular meaning. It constitutes for them part of the long search for that survival which has always been central to Judaism through the ages. Now the quest for statehood by Palestinians — Christian and Muslim — as part of their search for survival as a people in the Land, also calls for full attention.

2.17: Jews, Christians and Muslims have all maintained a presence in the Land from their beginnings. While "the Holy Land" is primarily a Christian designation, the Land is holy to all three. Although they may understand its holiness in different ways, it cannot be said to be "more holy" to one than to another.

2.18: The need for dialogue is the more urgent when under strain the dialogue is tested. Is it mere debate and negotiation or is it grounded in faith that God's will for the world is secure peace with justice and compassion?

3. Hatred and persecution of Jews — a continuing concern

3.1: Christians cannot enter into dialogue with Jews without the awareness that hatred and persecution of Jews have a long persistent history, especially in countries where Jews constitute a minority among Christians. The tragic history of the persecution of Jews includes massacres in Europe and the Middle East by the Crusaders, the Inquisition, pogroms, and the Holocaust. The World Council of Churches Assembly at its first meeting in Amsterdam, 1948, declared: "We call upon the churches we represent to denounce antisemitism, no matter what its origin, as absolutely irreconcilable with the profession and practice of the Christian faith. Antisemitism is sin against God and man." This appeal has been reiterated many times. Those who live where there is a record of acts of hatred against Jews can serve the whole Church by unmasking the ever-present danger they have come to recognize.

3.2: Teachings of contempt for Jews and Judaism in certain Christian traditions proved a spawning ground for the evil of the Nazi Holocaust.

The Church must learn so to preach and teach the Gospel as to make sure that it cannot be used towards contempt for Judaism and against the Jewish people. A further response to the Holocaust by Christians, and one which is shared by their Jewish partners, is a resolve that it will never happen again to the Jews or to any other people.

3.3: Discrimination against and persecution of Jews have deep-rooted socio-economic and political aspects. Religious differences are magnified to justify ethnic hatred in support of vested interests. Similar phenomena are also evident in many inter-racial conflicts. Christians should oppose all such religious prejudices, whereby people are made scapegoats for the failures and problems of societies and political regimes.

3.4: Christians in parts of the world with a history of little or no persecution of Jews do not wish to be conditioned by the specific experiences of justified guilt among other Christians. Rather, they explore in their own ways the significance of Jewish-Christian relations, from the earliest times to the present, for their life and witness.

4. Authentic Christian witness

4.1: Christians are called to witness to their faith in word and deed. The Church has a mission and it cannot be otherwise. This mission is not one of choice.

4.2: Christians have often distorted their witness by coercive proselytism — conscious and unconscious, overt and subtle. Referring to proselytism between Christian churches, the Joint Working Group of the Roman Catholic Church and the World Council of Churches stated: "Proselytism embraces whatever violates the right of the human person, Christian or non-Christian, to be free from external coercion in religious matters" (*The Ecumenical Review*, No.1, 1971, p.11).

4.3: Such rejection of proselytism, and such advocacy of respect for the integrity and the identity of all persons and all communities of faith, are urgent in relation to Jews, especially those who live as minorities among Christians. Steps towards assuring non-coercive practices are of highest importance. In dialogue ways should be found for the exchange of concerns, perceptions, and safeguards in these matters.

4.4: While Christians agree that there can be no place for coercion of any kind, they do disagree — on the basis of their understandings of the Scriptures — as to what constitutes authentic forms of mission. There is a wide spectrum, from those who see the very presence of the Church in the world as the witness called for, to those who see mission as the explicit and organized proclamation of the gospel to all who have not accepted Jesus as their Saviour.

4.5: This spectrum as to mission in general is represented in the different views of what is authentic mission to Jews. Here some of the specifics are as follows: There are Christians who view a mission to the Jews as having a very special salvific significance, and those who believe the conversion of the Jews to be the eschatological event that will climax the history of the world. There are those who would place no special emphasis on a mission to the Jews, but would include them in the one mission to all those who have not accepted Christ as their Saviour. There are those who believe that a mission to the Jews is not part of an authentic Christian witness, since the Jewish people finds its fulfilment in faithfulness to God's covenant of old.

4.6: Dialogue can rightly be described as a mutual witness, but only when the intention is to hear the others in order better to understand their faith, hopes, insights, and concerns, and to give, to the best of one's ability, one's own understanding of one's own faith. The spirit of dialogue is to be fully present to one another in full openness and human vulnerability.

4.7: According to rabbinic law, Jews who confess Jesus as the Messiah are considered apostate Jews. But for many Christians of Jewish origin, their identification with the Jewish people is a deep spiritual reality to which they seek to give expression in various ways, some by observing parts of Jewish tradition in worship and life-style, many by a special commitment to the wellbeing of the Jewish people and to a peaceful and secure future for the State of Israel. Among Christians of Jewish origin there is the same wide spectrum of attitudes towards mission as among other Christians, and the same criteria for dialogue and against coercion apply.

4.8: As Christians of different traditions enter into dialogue with Jews in local, national, and international situations, they will come to express their understanding of Judaism in other language, style, and ways than has been done in these Ecumenical Considerations. Such understandings are to be shared among the churches for enrichment of all.

● From: *Current Dialogue* No. 4, winter 1982-83, pp.5-12.

Document 8

The Sixth Assembly
of the World Council of Churches

The Assembly, held at Vancouver from 24 July to 10 August 1983, passed a more extensive "Statement on the Middle East", including the topics "the Israeli-Palestinian conflict", "Lebanon", and "Jerusalem".

The increasingly dangerous stituation in the Middle East threatens the peace of the whole world and places heavy demands on all those striving for justice and freedom.

The Middle East is a region of special interest as the birthplace of three monotheistic religions. The churches in the area have their roots from apostolic times. Their continued presence and active participation in the life of the whole area, despite suffering at various periods, is a remarkable witness to the faith. They are facing new challenges and attempting to respond through new forms of witness. While only the churches of the Middle East can determine the nature and forms of their witness, it behoves all churches to strengthen their presence and support their ministry, especially the ministry of reconciliation and witness for peace. Historical factors and certain theological interpretations have often confused Christians outside in evaluating the religious and political developments in the Middle East.

Recent developments in the region have further pushed back prospects for peace. The agony of the Lebanese war is not yet over. The integrity and independence of Lebanon are in greater danger than ever. The Israeli settlement policy on the West bank has resulted in a *de facto* annexation, giving final touches to a discriminatory policy of development of peoples that flagrantly violates the basic rights of the Palestinian people. There are fears of relocation of the inhabitants of the West Bank and their expulsion. A large number of Palestinians are under detention in the prisons on the West Bank and in camps in Lebanon. There is escalation of tension in the occupied territories. The consensus among the Arab nations appears to have been lost. External and internal pressures have caused serious rift within the Palestinian movement. In many situations there are increasing violations of human rights, especially of minorities, and religious fanaticism is a bane of many communities. The Iran-Iraqi war continues to claim an increasing toll of lives and complicates inter-Arab relations. Tension is increasing in relation to Cyprus.

The Israeli-Palestinian conflict

We reaffirm the principles previously enunciated by the WCC as the basis on which a peaceful settlement can be reached. The UN Security Council Resolution 242 and all other relevant UN resolutions need to be revised and implemented, taking into account changes that have occurred since 1967, and such revisions should express the following principles in a manner that would ensure:

a) the withdrawal of Israeli troops from all territories occupied in 1967;
b) the right of all states, including Israel and Arab states, to live in peace with secure and recognized boundaries;
c) the implementation of the rights of the Palestinians to self-determination, including the right of establishing a sovereign Palestinian state.

We reaffirm that the Middle East conflict cannot be resolved through the use of force but only through peaceful means. Negotiations for a comprehensive settlement in the Middle East should include all those parties most intimately involved: the State of Israel, the Palestine Liberation Organization and neighbouring Arab states. The interests of the world at large are best represented through the United Nations, and the USA and the USSR have a special responsibility in this matter.

Churches should undertake the following with a view to facilitating processes towards negotiations:

a) to build greater awareness among the churches about the urgency and justice of the Palestinian cause. In this connection active support should be extended to the UN International Conference on the Question of Palestine to be held at the end of August 1983 in Geneva. The churches should bring to bear their influence on states to participate in it;
b) to encourage the dialogue between Palestinians and Israelis with a view to furthering mutual understanding and enabling recognition;

c) to remind Christians in the Western world to recognize that their guilt over the fate of Jews in their countries may have influenced their views of the conflict in the Middle East and has often led to uncritical support of the policies of the State of Israel, thereby ignoring the plight of the Palestinian people and their rights. In this context we welcome the more open and critical stance adopted by Christian churches in the traditional Jewish-Christian dialogue, but we also urge the broadening of the dialogue to include larger segments of both Christian and Jewish communities;

d) to support movements within Israel, which are working for peace and reconciliation.

Lebanon

The ecumenical community shares the agony of the peoples in Lebanon who have been tragically suffering over the last nine years and who have been carrying too large a burden of the problems of the region.

We reiterate that the recovery of Lebanese territorial integrity and sovereignty is a key to peace and justice in the region and that for this to be realized all foreign forces must be withdrawn from Lebanese territory.

We appeal to the ecumenical community:

a) to support the efforts of the Lebanese government to reassert the effective exercise of its sovereignty over all Lebanese territory and to support full independence and unity of the Lebanese people;

b) to assist the churches within Lebanon in their attempts with leaders of the religious communities for reconciliation, with a view to achieving harmony and unity among all communities in the country;

c) to continue to support generously the Middle East Council of Churches and the churches in Lebanon in their humanitarian and social programmes of relief for all in Lebanon;

d) to collaborate with the churches in the area in their contribution to the promotion of justice, dignity, freedom and human rights for all in Lebanon.

Jerusalem

We reaffirm that "Jerusalem is a Holy City for three monotheistic religions: Judaism, Christianity and Islam. The tendency to minimize Jerusalem's importance for any of these three religions should be avoided" (WCC Fifth Assembly, Nairobi, 1975). The WCC should implement the proposal of the WCC Central Committee (August 1980) that dialogue be initiated with Jews and Muslims so that members of the three religions can understand each other's deep religious attachment to Jerusalem and so that together they can contribute towards political processes that would lead to a mutually acceptable agreement for sharing the city. The churches should give priority to this while continuing efforts to secure a general settlement of the Middle East conflicts. The special legislation known as the Status Quo of the Holy Places must be safeguarded and confirmed in any agreement concerning Jerusalem.

a) We call the attention of the churches to the need for:
   — actions which will ensure a continuing indigenous Christian presence and witness in Jerusalem;
   — wider ecumenical awareness of the plight of the indigenous Muslim and Christian communities suffering from the repressive action of the occupying power in East Jerusalem and other occupied territories.

b) We call upon all churches to express their common concern that although Israeli law guarantees free access for members of all religious traditions rooted in Jerusalem to their holy places, the state of war between Israel and Arab states, the political reality created by the Israeli annexation of East Jerusalem and continuing occupation of the West Bank means that Arab Muslims and Christians continue to experience serious difficulties and are often prevented from visiting the Holy City.

We uphold the churches in the Middle East in our intercessions as they respond to the new challenges in the difficult circumstances through their witness in the service of Christ. We assure them of the solidarity of the community of faith around the world as we have gathered together here in the name of Jesus Christ the Life of the World. We pray for the healing of the wounds in the nations of that region.

We stand together with other religious communities in a spirit of servanthood seeking to be faithful in our common calling to be peacemakers and reconcilers and to bring hope for all.

● From: *Gathered for Life*, ed. David Gill, Geneva, WCC, 1983, pp.147-151.

Document 9

Synod of the Evangelical Church in Germany

The Synod of the Evangelical Church in Germany (Evangelische Kirche in Deutschland), which at that time included both parts of Germany, held at Berlin-Weissensee from 23 to 27 April 1950, passed a "Statement on the Jewish Question" ("Wort zur Judenfrage"), which is also frequently referred to as "Statement of Guilt regarding Israel" ("Wort zur Schuld an Israel").

For God has consigned all men to disobedience, that he may have mercy upon all (Rom. 11:32).

We believe in the Lord and Saviour, who as a person came from the people of Israel.

We confess the Church which is joined together in one body of Jewish Christians and Gentile Christians and whose peace is Jesus Christ.

We believe God's promise to be valid for his Chosen People even after the crucifixion of Jesus Christ.

We state that by omission and silence we became implicated before the God of mercy in the outrage which has been perpetrated against the Jews by people of our nation.

We caution all Christians not to balance what has come upon us as God's judgment against what we have done to the Jews; for in judgment God's mercy searches the repentant.

We ask all Christians to dissociate themselves from all antisemitism and earnestly to resist it, wherever it stirs again, and to encounter Jews and Jewish Christians in a brotherly spirit.

We ask the Christian congregations to protect Jewish graveyards within their areas if they are unprotected.

We pray to the Lord of mercy that he may bring about the Day of Completion when we will be praising the triumph of Jesus Christ together with the saved Israel.

● From: *Kirchliches Jahrbuch für die Evangelische Kirche in Deutschland 1950*, Gütersloh, 1951, pp.5f. English translation: RR.

Document 10

Netherlands Reformed Church

In its constitution, adopted in May 1951, the Netherlands Reformed Church was the first church body in history to include a special section on the dialogue with Israel as different from the mission to the Gentiles.

VIII. On the apostolate of the Church

1. As a Christ-confessing community of faith, placed in the world in order to bear witness of God's promises and commandments before all men and every power, in the hope of the kingdom of God the Church carries out her apostolic commission, in particular:
— by her dialogue with Israel;
— by the work of mission;
— by spreading the gospel and by continuous efforts towards the Christianizing of people's life in the spirit of the Reformation.

2. In the dialogue with Israel the Church turns to the synagogue and to all who belong to the Chosen People in order to bear witness to them from the holy scripture, that Jesus is the Christ.

3. In the work of mission the church goes with the gospel of the kingdom to the people in the non-Christian world, in obedience to the command of Christ and in pursuance of the service of mercy in spiritual and physical need; she carries out the service of mercy in the spiritual and physical need of these peoples; by ministry of word and sacrament she gathers into congregations those who have attained the faith and received holy baptism; she serves those congregations by establishing and building up an indigenous church life; in all these ways she also works towards a Christianization of the society.

4. In spreading the gospel to those who are alienated from the gospel the Church seeks to bring them back into community with Christ and his Church; in all her subdivisions she struggles for a reformational character of nation and people, and in the hope of the kingdom of God, her efforts towards its Christianization are directed to the authorities and the people so as to orientate life according to the promises and commandments of God.

● From: *Kerkorde der Nederlandse Hervormde Kerk*, Voekencentrum, 's Gravenhage, 1956, pp.11f. English translation: RR.

Document 11

General Synod of the Netherlands Reformed Church

In June 1970 the General Synod of the Netherlands Reformed Church adopted an extensive study document on "Israel: People, Land and State". Below is given the text of chapters II "The Jewish People in the Old Testament", V "The State of Israel", and VI "Epilogue".

II. The Jewish People in the Old Testament

Israel is in its historical reality the chosen people

5. The Israel about which the OT speaks was in fact in the world. It consisted of men of flesh and blood, who dwelt in a certain land and had a visible history with treaties, wars, victories and defeats.

6. However, according to this people's testimony of faith, upon which also, thanks to Christ, our faith as Christians is built, it was a people unlike all other peoples. The fact is exclusively based on God's election. He promised that it would be a people before it existed — and only afterwards did it become a people. He assigned it a land with which it was not connected by nature — and afterwards it came into this land. He made a covenant with it and made known to it his will, and this became the tie which bound it together as a people.

7. Therefore the Jewish people of the OT are as a historical reality, the elected people. Here the elective acts of God, which are based on nothing but his sovereign love, obtained a visible form upon this earth amidst the nations. Here it has become clear that God's election is not a mere idea, but that it enters the world in all concreteness. Therefore this people has to be considered from two points of view: (1) Historically it is a people

subject to human failure and all the vicissitudes of history. (2) Because it is the people to whom God has bound himself in a special way, in the history of Israel we are somehow indirectly dealing with God. It is in it that he reveals himself to faith.

8. God had chosen his people for himself; he had formed it and set it apart. This was known by Israel and testified to in its faith. But there was always the danger that it might separate this act of election from the God who elected. Then it regarded the election as a possession on which it could count; and then it was necessary for the prophets to remind their people that their being chosen was based solely on the free grace of God. Israel should know that it could never lay claim to this grace of God as if it were a right. But Israel was also to know that its God was faithful and dependable. Therefore it could trust him, who had made it his chosen people. That is to say, we cannot set faith in the electing God in opposition to the grateful and wondering recognition of being-elected. Election as the free act of God and being-elected, as the being-determined by this act, belong together: the latter is the converse of the former.

9. In its testimonies of faith Israel understood its election as a gift of grace. In many passages of the OT there is a note of grateful wonder about the great privilege of being the special treasure of God and knowing him and his will (cf. Ex. 19:5,6). But the prophets in particular continuously reminded their people that this privilege carried with it a special responsibility; Israel should walk according to righteousness; its privilege should be a blessing to the nations. Its election was both gift and task. Israel was not to forget that its God is the God of the whole earth and of all nations, and that in his love God wants to disclose himself to all. In that light the people were to see their election.

The Land

10. In its faith Israel regarded its tie with the land as a unique one. It had no natural right to the land, and was not allowed to deal with it as if the land were its possession to which it could lay claim. It was the land allotted by God to his people, the land which God had already promised to the patriarchs. Even in a time when Israel dwelt already in the land and had possession of it, it remained the "promised land", the gift of grace which was inseparably bound up with God's love. In other words, Israel was always convinced that the land was an essential element of the covenant.

11. According to the entire OT in all its parts the chosen people and the promised land belong together, owing to God. The land was the place

allotted to this people in order that they might realize their vocation as God's people to form a holy society. Again and again the prophets stress the point that the land is promised and given for the sake of this calling. When the people did not come up to their vocation as a chosen people, the prophets threatened them with expulsion. Exile was understood by them as a sign of divine judgment, and return was understood as God's renewed gracious turning towards his people and as a new possibility, granted by him, for them to live according to their calling. Being allowed to dwell in the land could be regarded as a visible sign of God's election and as a concrete form of salvation.

12. We have said above that for Israel its election was no end in itself, but was directed towards the future: through the fulfilment of the destiny of the people of God and through what God does to his people, the nations also shall get to know God and shall turn to him. The dwelling of Israel in the land also partook of this directedness towards the future. This perspective in which the promised land is put comes clearly to the fore in the preaching of the prophets in the time of the exile. When they speak about the return to the land, they have in mind the historical situation; however, they speak in terms which go far beyond the historical, actual moment. It was the firm conviction of the people of the OT that they could reach their real destiny as God's covenant-people only in the land of Palestine and that the realization of this destiny was closely linked to the salvation of the world.

13. Thus according to the OT the land forms an essential part of the election, by which God has bound himself to this particular people. Certainly the bond of God with his people is not severed when the people are outside the land, and certainly the people can live there also in quiet and peace, but the enforced separation of people and land is always something abnormal. There is no question of a separate election of the land; rather, it is a vital aspect of the election of Israel. This cannot, however, be said of the city of Jerusalem, or of the kingship, or of the independent state. Whatever value may have been attached to them in particular times, they were not inherent in Israel's election. Concerning Jerusalem, the special importance of the city is based on four elements according to the OT. First, it is the place in which God has chosen to be present in his sanctuary amidst his people. The election of the city (e.g. 1 Kings 8; 2 Kings 21; 2 Chron. 6:5) is determined by the fact that God wants his name to be in the temple of Zion. Second, Jerusalem derives its significance from the fact that it is the city of the Davidic kingship since the election of David. Furthermore, in certain

OT passages Jerusalem is a symbol for the whole land and the whole people. Finally, there are passages which ascribe to Jerusalem an eschatological significance.

14. Nor was the historical kingship an essential element of the election of OT Israel. The very fact that it came into existence at a relatively late date and amidst strong prophetic criticism is proof of this. This kingship can truly express the sovereignty of God over his people, but it can also be an abandonment of God. Therefore since its beginning it always had a certain ambivalence. And the fact that the people had no state of their own played no decisive role as long as foreign rulers let them live in quiet and peace in their own land and did not prevent them from living according to the order willed by God.

Identity and alienation

15. According to their own OT witness the Jewish people as a whole were called to be God's covenant people. Their vocation was to realize, as a national entity, in the land given to them for that purpose, a society in which only God's will was law, in order to mediate salvation to all nations. The true identity of Israel as God's people lay in its being determined by its election; it is characterized by three inter-related elements: the reception of God's revelation, the dwelling in the "promised land" in order to form a holy society, and its universal significance.

16. The people in their totality were not faithful to their identity. The prophets vehemently accuse Israel of refusing to listen to God's word when they call it to repentance. Again and again the OT speaks of Israel's defection and disobedience. This mirrors our own alienation from God. Therefore it should be a matter of wonder and gratefulness for all men that the unfaithful people did not lose their vocation as covenant-people. That this did not happen is due to God's election, which cannot be nullified. Therefore Israel still shows signs of its vocation even in its alienation. God in his election puts his mark upon Israel as his covenant-people, and this is a visible mark.

17. The OT testifies to Israel's alienation; however, simultaneously the book itself is a sign of Israel's identity. For these writings are written in, and have been preserved and collected by, this people, which itself is constantly criticized in them. The very existence of the OT — these books by which the church also lives — is a sign of Israel's vocation to be a blessing to all nations.

18. In respect of content, there is a manifest tension between the true and the false prophets, between those who understood the unique revela-

tion of their unique God and those who confused it with and linked it to their own wishes or the religions of the nations. In the centuries after the Babylonian exile, groups of the pious were formed, who separated themselves from the great masses; in practice this meant that they withdrew from the masses and that they relinquished the idea that in Israel nation and congregation should be identical. And while some held fast to the universal vocation of their people, as particularly the great prophets of former times had expressed it, others wanted to preserve the nation as a holy and separate community, in such a way that they lost sight of this vocation.

V. The State of Israel

The significance of the return

41. We have spoken about the unique destiny of the Jews to be God's covenant people and about the unique tie which binds them and the land of Palestine together. Even the rejection of Jesus Christ did not bring any change in this regard. Thereby the people indeed affirmed their alienation which they had shown already, but they are still the chosen people, destined to fulfill a lasting and separate role. In our time many Jews have again gone to the land of Palestine. In this way the people, who were threatened with disappearance, partly through assimilation, partly through awful pogroms and acts of extermination, have again obtained a new, clearly visible form. Precisely in its concrete visibility, this return points to the special significance of this people in the midst of the nations, and to the saving faithfulness of God; it is a sign for us that it is God's will to be on earth together with man. Therefore we rejoice in this reunion of people and land.

42. However, we do not intend to imply that the return is the final stage of history, nor that the people can never again be expelled from the land. Indeed, in the return the grace of God's lasting election has become manifest, but this return carries with it a special threat. For it could be that the other peoples deny a place to the Jews who are in their midst. It could also be that Israel does not use the new chance which it has received to fulfill its destiny in the land. But both these perils cannot prevent us from understanding the return positively as a confirmation of God's lasting purpose with his people.

The relative necessity of the State

43. However, the issue is not merely the return but also the state. God's promise applies to the lasting tie of people and land, but not in the same

way to the tie of people and state. In biblical times the Jewish people have lived for centuries in Palestine without having an independent state of their own. It is also possible that in the future circumstances will be such that the Jews as an entity can live unhindered in their land without forming a specifically Jewish state, or even that they can fulfill their vocation better if they are part of a larger whole. But as matters are at the moment, we see a free state as the only possibility which safeguards the existence of the people and which offers them the chance to be truly themselves. The former hope of some for a bi-national state in the full sense of the word, seems in the present situation not possible to realize. For right after the second world war a great influx of Jewish refugees disrupted the precarious equilibrium of Jews and Arabs. That seems to preclude the possibility of a bi-national state, at least for the moment, to say nothing of the existing hostility between Arabs and Jews. Another possibility, which is sometimes mentioned, that of a federation in Palestine, presupposes at least that peace should first be made. Finally there is the possibility which the Arab countries offer the Jews, namely to accept a minority position in a Muslim state. But this would imply that in the promised land the Jewish ghetto with its attendant mentality and dangers would be continued. Therefore we are convinced that everyone who accepts the reunion of the Jewish people and the land for reasons of faith, has also to accept that in the given circumstances the people should have a state of their own.

The state and the special place of the Jewish people
44. Because of the special place of the Jewish people we endorse in the present situation the right of existence of the State of Israel. On the other hand we wonder whether this same special place does not also make this right questionable. First of all, we remember the way in which the state came into existence in 1948. This took place in a human, all too human way, as is the case with practically every other state; all kinds of political means and often means of violence have been used. But the Jewish people have never been better than other peoples. The entry in the land under Joshua and the return under Nehemia were, morally speaking, dubious affairs too. The special place of Israel was never based on its moral qualities, but solely on what in the OT is called God's righteousness, that is his unmerited, steadfast covenant-love. This love can never be a licence to sin. But it is not annulled by sin either. Therefore we ought not to dispute on moral grounds the right of the State of Israel to exist. Otherwise we would have to ask ourselves how we ourselves can stand before God.

45. In the second place we must ask whether the universal purpose of Israel's election does not exclude the possibility of a state of their own. Indeed, the state carries with it the temptation for this people to become a nation like the other nations. The existence of a state can easily lead to an attitude of isolation, rivalry and defensiveness; and if this took place, then Israel could not fulfill its calling to be a bridge between separate peoples (Is. 19:23-25). But this far from imaginary danger is not necessarily inherent in the existence of a state. A state means concentration and structuralization of national life, but not necessarily isolation. In the present situation at least, a state gives greater opportunity to the Jews to fulfill their vocation than any alternative can offer.

46. Therefore we maintain that whoever accepts for the Jewish people a role of their own among the nations must also in view of the political problems in and around Palestine accept for this people the right to a state of their own. Because this acceptance is based on the lasting tie with the land in virtue of the promise, i.e. because it is ultimately based on reasons of faith, it cannot be a matter of *uncommitted* discussion in the Christian community. Otherwise one takes the risk of divorcing the NT from the OT, God from history, and his commandment from his promise; that would mean a de-spiritualization and de-moralization of the Christian faith.

The vocation and ambiguity of the state

47. Because the the special place in which by divine decree the Jews stand, the State of Israel also has a dimension of its own. The election of the people implies the vocation to realize their peoplehood in an exemplary way. Therefore, the state also has to be exemplary. Israel is called to live in its state in such a manner that a new understanding of what a state is, is enacted before the eyes of the other peoples. But those who among Israel plead for this exemplary existence find little response at the present time. In the state also there is manifest the brokenness and ambiguity to which the entire history of the Jewish people witness.

48. The land is given to Israel as dwelling place; there it can have its state. But the boundaries of this state cannot be read from the Bible. The territory in which the Jewish people lived in OT times has had very different boundaries, and these never coincided with those of which the prophetic promises spoke. The only thing of which we are sure is that these boundaries must be such that they offer the Jewish people a dwelling place where they can be themselves. But it is a matter of a dwelling place, not a sphere of power and control. The necessity of

protecting their dwelling place should not induce the Jews to make it into a nationalistic state in which the only thing that counts is military power. It is true that the so-called Christian states also have frequently succumbed to this temptation. But this is exactly the point, namely that in this way Israel is in danger of becoming a people like all other peoples, not worse and not better. Such a collective assimilation would be a denial of its true nature.

49. The Jewish people are called to exercise justice in an exemplary way. This too is an essential aspect of their true identity. In this respect the problems caused by the founding of the State of Israel and its later military victories are a particular challenge for the people. Hundreds of thousands of Palestinian refugees live miserably, without rights, around the borders of Israel. It belongs to Israel's vocation that it should know itself to be responsible for them and that it should do all it can to put right the injustice done to them. This is possible only if it were to search for a political solution which would not be based on violence, as is mostly the case among the other peoples, but which would be based on justice and true humanity.

50. According to the biblical witness God promised the land to his people at a time when other peoples lived there. Israel could never lay claim to the land by right. It was not allowed to consider it as its own possession. It had to learn, and to show others, what it means to live in a land by the grace of God. Hence comes the OT commandment to treat the foreigner in its midst as if he were a fellow Jew. Now, in our own time, Israel is offered the chance to establish a form of government which guarantees its own Jewish existence, and which at the same time respects the full freedom and dignity of its non-Jewish fellow citizens. But in spite of rights which are officially granted, these non-Jewish people are actually treated as second class citizens. It may be true that at the moment weighty reasons of political expediency can be given for this discrimination. But it is not in accordance with Israel's calling.

Jerusalem

51. Through its specific development Jerusalem offers Israel an outstanding opportunity to practise a new, non-nationalistic and non-exclusive way of thinking. This city, which because of its history has great meaning for many Christians and Muslims, ought to be a kind of experimental garden where various nations may live together in peace. But as soon as we state this, questions arise which we cannot answer unanimously. Has the city become the concentrated expression of the

union of land and people to such a degree that, if by reason of faith one supports the right of Israel to live in its land, one also has to include an affirmation of the lasting tie between this people and its city? Or can the exemplary function of Jerusalem as a city of peace, to which all nations can go up, be realized fully only if the city were internationalized and made independent of all other states? Or should one plead for a status of its own for Jerusalem within Israel, in order that around this city the state may develop into a state which is really a blessing for all nations and states? We have no clear and unanimous answer to these questions. But we believe that the problems concerning the city of Jerusalem call for a solution by Israel in a new framework of political thinking.

Election as calling and as offence

52. In speaking of Israel's unfaithfulness to its special calling, we did not assume that we are better than the Jews. We are only too conscious of the fact that we too as Christians, as churches, as so-called Christian states have repeatedly been guilty of discrimination, inhumanity and impermissible forms of nationalism. If Israel were a state like other states, we would not judge it by standards which no other state meets. But we believe that Israel is unique; its nature is based on God's election, for the Jews are still that special people which by God's promises is tied to this particular land. Therefore we expect from this people more than we expect from any other people. He who is placed in a special position has to act in a special manner.

53. Many Jews are not at all eager to be placed in an exceptional position and to have to solve the problems which the State of Israel poses, in a way to which the other peoples do not yet live up. And indeed, their special position has often seemed offensive to the Jews themselves. In view of what has been said above about identity and alienation this can hardly be surprising. But even when the Jewish people in their public life do not yet really meet the demands of their destiny, we are not justified in rejecting the right of existence for their state. For that right is based on God's preserving the identity of his people even in their alienation, and on his dealing with them in a special way.

VI. Epilogue

Church and Israel

54. Israel's way through history is interconnected with the expectation of the church and, therefore, as Christians we cannot be silent about

Israel. The full realization of the identity of Israel would mean that the Jewish people would truly accept God's coming in their midst. But this would be the same thing as to accept Jesus Christ as the one in whom God has affirmed and fulfilled the covenant with his people. The actual acceptance of Christ would open the way to the complete fulfilment of God's purpose with the world, to the kingdom of God, in which the difference between Jews and Gentiles would no longer be of any account. But as long as we still live in a transitional state, this side of the fulfilment, God will preserve, side by side with the church, the Jewish people as a visible sign of his electing faithfulness.

55. In this time before the ultimate fulfilment, we as the church are called together with the people of Israel to be true to our vocation. The difference between us is that our starting point is the way of Jesus Christ, who is not yet recognized by Israel as the fulfilment of *its* destiny. But we ourselves also do not live truly and entirely on the basis of the salvation which we have received. Indeed, if we were to live in that way, the Jews would be made jealous. The fact that does not happen shows how imperfectly the church fulfills her calling; the criticism which we make against the Jewish people comes back upon our own heads. The Christian church too has not yet reached her destiny, she too lives still in a transitional state. The Jewish people and the church are both travellers and both are preserved, each in its own way, in God's faithfulness.

● From: *Israel: Land, Volk en Staat*, Handreiking voor een theologische bezin-ning, Voekencentrum, 's Gravenhage, 1971. English translation: H. Croner ed., *Stepping Stones to Further Jewish-Christian Relations*, London, Stimulus Books, Vol. 1, 1977, pp.91-107.

General Conference of the
United Methodist Church (USA)

In 1972 the General Conference of the United Methodist Church in the USA adopted a "Statement on Inter-religious Dialogue: Jews and Christians" which includes specific recommendations for the dialogue

Common roots

1. The United Methodist Church understands itself to be a part of the people of God and specifically a part of the whole Christian church, the body of Christ. It also gives thanks for its roots in historic Judaism. It rejoices in the reciprocal patrimony of the Old and New Testaments.

The heritage and hopes of a religious Israel in the context of which Jesus labored have continued to live in the Jewish faith and people. Christian awareness of indebtedness, however, to that history and its relationship to God is not as clear as it ought to be. Not only is the God we worship the same and many of our ethical concerns are held in common, but there are also numerous traditions in Israel's history whose impact upon and potential for the Christian church were lost or are still undiscovered. Moreover, to be faithful to Jesus the Jew, the contemporary relationship of United Methodist Christians and those who worship as Jews should not be neglected.

Appreciation for common roots should not blind us to the fundamental and inherently mutual theological problems to be faced. The relationship between the covenant of God with Israel and the covenant made in Jesus Christ and the understandings by Jew and Christian of each of these covenants merits exploration anew. Openness to the blessing of God on all covenanted people may lead to useful penetration of the intricacies of the interfaith discussions, if not to ultimate solutions. Serious new conversations need not and should not require either Jews or Christians to sacrifice their convictions. There is rich opportunity for potential growth in mutual understanding.

Service for humanity

2. At this moment in history, the potential of our common heritage is particularly important for the advancement of causes decisive for the survival of all mankind. While it is true that the concept of human brotherhood and solidarity is not represented by Jews or Christians alone, this concept has been central for both from their beginnings. The sacredness of persons as God's creation is expressed clearly in both the Old and New Testaments. The biblical view of each human being as an intrinsic member of the community of persons forbids any suppression of groups through society at large and any manipulation of individuals as well. Nevertheless, Jews in particular have been victims of systematic oppression and injustice more recurrently and more barbarously than have Christians. Therefore, in order to continue Jewish and Christian effort for the common cause of mankind, it is not enough for contemporary Christians to be aware of our common origins. Christians must also become aware of that history in which they have deeply alienated the Jews. They are obliged to examine their own implicit and explicit responsibility for the discrimination against and for organized extermination of Jews, as in the recent past. The persecution by Christians of Jews throughout centuries calls for clear repentance and resolve to repudiate past injustice and to seek its elimination in the present. In provision of guidelines for action and in specific processes of reconciling action for all men there is an opportunity now to join hands with Jews in common cause for a human community.

For Jew and Christian alike, God is active in history. The political and social orders are not free from his judgment. Dialogue which does not blink at differences of assumptions and interpretations of scripture and faith, but which accentuates the fundamental agreements for the sake of service to society can be, in the providence of God, a timely and fruitful inter-religious adventure.

Exploring together

3. In many areas of spiritual and intellectual concern the past relationship of Jews and Christians has been vitiated by inadequate communication. We have talked past one another instead of with each other. In new conversations there is an important opportunity to move past the polemi-

cal use of scripture and to explore how and why past conditioning keeps us apart, while we have much in common. In such dialogues, an aim of religious or political conversion, or of proselytizing, cannot be condoned.

To commend the love of God in Jesus Christ through saving word and serving work is an ingredient of dialogue for Christians, but antisemitism (against Jew or Arab) represents a denial of the love we proclaim and compromises our service of justice. Fruitful discussions should proceed with the clear acknowledgment that there is no valid biblical or theological basis for antisemitism. Prejudice and discrimination on racial grounds are not valid expressions of Christian faith. Why people still violate their unity given in God, and in his creation and redemption, should be examined in company with our Jewish brothers and sisters.

Responsibility in problem areas

4. Dialogues presently are complicated by problems of scriptural interpretation, conditioned attitudes, and turbulent political struggles such as the search for Jewish and Arab security and dignity in the Middle East. Facing these difficulties together may lead to creative results. In this process, we are obligated to respect the right of the Jews, as of all religious groups, to interpret their own scripture with regard to their peoplehood and destiny. When rival political positions each claim scriptural warrant, however, the issues no longer are related simply to religious freedom for one or another but to the political issue of how resources may be distributed justly. In Jewish-Christian dialogues is placed a responsibility for being concerned for the implications in the Middle East for peace and justice for all persons.

The Christian obligation to those who survived the Nazi Holocaust, the understanding of the relationship of land and peoplehood, and the conviction that God loves all persons, suggest that a new dimension in dialogue with Jews is needed. A new perspective for Christians is a prerequisite for the reduction of mutual ignorance and distrust.

Guidelines for conversations

5. The principles which have been outlined above implicitly or explicitly suggest some practical guidelines which can instruct conversations in local communities and at other points of interaction. An incomplete list of the more important considerations is attempted here.

a) Wherever possible, conversations with members of Jewish communities should be initiated and maintained through an existing or an ad hoc ecumenical framework. The ecumenical body could begin by accepting the principles in this United Methodist statement as a foundation for the dialogue, or by drafting its own.

b) In the absence of cooperative Christian efforts to explore mutual understanding, tensions and difficulties, United Methodist initiative (or response to Jewish initiative) is to be encouraged.

c) Christian participants should make clear that they do not justify past injustice done by Christians to Jews and that there is no tenable biblical or theological base for antisemitism, and that they themselves wish to be free of it.

d) Joint planning of conversations should emphasize the broad purposes of dialogues and lessen suspicion that conversion is a deliberate intention.

e) Honest differences should be expected and probed seriously, even as areas of agreement and mutual support are discovered.

f) A series of meetings with some guarantee of continuity of participants is necessary for fruitful conversation. False hopes and superficial optimism resulting from a single session together can lead to despair and further alienation.

g) The joint study of that part of our tradition which both groups have in common, the Jewish Bible or the Christian Old Testament, can be of paramount importance. It is here that the foundations of Jewish and Christian existence coincide. A joint study has potential for new insights into our mutual relationship and our togetherness.

h) Conversations which begin with exploration of scriptural and traditional heritages may move to political and sociological and economic investigations and might well result in common action in the cause of human rights.

i) The dialogues should not overlook the rich opportunities afforded in visitation of synagogues and churches and in common prayer and other inter-religious services.

Declaration of intent

6. No one can see with absolute clarity the shape of the future. Openness to dialogue with other major religions of the world is not excluded for the future, but a bond of understanding and peace between Jew and Christian surely is one key ingredient of a viable community of persons. In both theological and practical issues of the moment there are offered challenges and opportunities for growth.

A reduction of Jewish or Christian beliefs to a tepid lowest common denominator of hardly distinguishable culture religions is not sought in this process. A new confrontation of our common roots, of our common potential for service to humanity, with the benefits from mutual explorations, and with the knotty contemporary problems of world peace commends itself to us. Thus, it is the desire of the United Methodist Church honestly and persistently to participate in conversations with Jews. Our intent includes commitment to their intrinsic worth and import for society. It includes as well the Christian hope that the "oneness given in Jesus Christ" may become an example of hope for the oneness of humanity. Within this framework and in acknowledgment of the common Fatherhood of God on all occasions for this new inter-religious adventure the United Methodist Church seeks to be responsive.

● From: *CCJP Newsletter*, No. 2, 1972, pp.4-7.

Document 13

General Convention
of the American Lutheran Church

In October 1974 the Seventh General Convention of the American Lutheran Church adopted a statement on "The American Lutheran Church and the Jewish Community" which in the preamble is called "a statement of comment and counsel addressed to the members of the congregations of the American Lutheran Church to aid them in their decisions and actions".

Preamble

There are many cogent reasons which urge us to reconsider the relationship of Lutherans, and indeed of all Christians, to Jews. Christians are not as aware as they should be of the common roots and origin of the church and the Jewish tradition of faith and life. Both Judaism and Christianity regard the Hebrew Bible — the Old Testament — as the document which bears witness to the beginning of God's saving work in history. They worship the same God and hold many ethical concerns in common, even though they are divided with respect to faith in Jesus of Nazareth as the Messiah.

Christians must also become aware of that history in which they have deeply alienated the Jews. It is undeniable that Christian people have both initiated and acquiesced in persecution. Whole generations of Christians have looked with contempt upon this people who were condemned to remain wanderers on the earth on the false charge of deicide. Christians ought to acknowledge with repentance and sorrow their part in this tragic history of estrangement. Since anti-Jewish prejudice is still alive in many parts of the world, Christians need to develop a sympathetic understanding of the renewal among Jews of the terror of the Holocaust. It is as if the numbness of the injury has worn off, old wounds have been reopened, and Jews live in dread of another disaster. Christians must join with Jews in the effort to understand the theological and moral significance of what happened in the Holocaust.

We need also to look to the future to see if there are things Christians and Jews can do together in service to the community. Better communication between Christians and Jews can lead to more adequate joint efforts on behalf of a humane society. The new atmosphere in theological research and interfaith encounter which has developed within recent years summons us to undertake serious conversations with Jewish people. Some Christians feel a special concern to explore the contribution which American churches might make in and through contacts with their Jewish neighbours and others to a resolution of the conflict in the Middle East that will be to the benefit of all those living in that region.

The urgency of the foregoing considerations is heightened by the fact that about 50 percent of all Jews live in North America. As Lutherans we ought, therefore, to regard our Jewish neighbours as major partners in the common life.

We urge that Lutherans should understand that their relationship to the Jewish community is one of solidarity, of confrontation, and of respect and cooperation.

I. Solidarity

Our common humanity

Lutherans and Jews, indeed all mankind, are united by virtue of their humanity. Lutherans and Jews agree that all people, regardless of race, religion or nationality, are equally God's children, and equally precious in his sight. This conviction is based on a concept of God as Creator of the universe, who continues to care for his creation, whose mercies are over all his creatures.

Our common heritage

The existence of Jewish congregations today shows that a religious tradition which traces its ancestry back to the time of Abraham is still living and growing. It is a tradition that gave rise to Christianity; a tradition from which Christianity has borrowed much. But modern Judaism has grown, changed, and developed considerably beyond the Judaism of biblical times, just as the modern church has grown, changed, and developed considerably beyond its New Testament beginnings.

It is unfortunate that so few Christians have studied Judaism as it grew and flowered in the centuries since the New Testament era. The first step for Lutherans, therefore, is to devote themselves to completing this long-neglected homework. It is strongly recommended that Lutherans ask the Jews themselves to teach them about this long and critically important period in Jewish history.

Our spiritual solidarity

Our solidarity is based on those ideas and themes held in common, most of which were inherited by Christianity from the Jewish tradition. It is important to note that the ministry of Jesus and the life of the early Christian community were thoroughly rooted in the Judaism of their day. To emphasize the Jewishness of Jesus and his disciples, and to stress all that binds Jews and Christians together in their mutual history is also to attack one of the sources of anti-Jewish prejudice. We are, after all, brothers one to another. Judaism and Christianity both worship the one God. We both call Abraham father. We both view ourselves as communities covenanted to God. We both feel called to serve in the world as God's witnesses and to be a blessing to mankind.

This emphasis on solidarity is not meant to ignore the many differences that exist between Lutherans and Jews. Rather it is through an understanding and appreciation of what we have in common that we can best discuss our differences. But for the moment, Lutherans have an obligation to fulfill — namely, to understand adequately and fairly the Jews and Judaism. This is the immediate purpose of Lutheran conversations with Jews.

It is hoped that as Lutherans better understand this similar, yet different religious tradition, the wounds of the past will be healed, and Lutherans and Jews together will be able to face the future receptive to the direction of the Holy Spirit as he seeks to accomplish the will of the One in whom all men live and move and have their being.

II. Confrontation

The history of separation and persecution

American Lutherans are the heirs of a long history of prejudicial discrimination against Jews, going back to pre-Christian times. The beginnings of this history of hate are obscure, but gross superstition and the desire for a scapegoat were prominent aspects. The separation between church and synagogue became final by the end of the first century. When Christianity was made the official religion of the Roman empire, a systematic degradation of Jews began in which both church and empire played their parts. Jews were regarded as enemies who were to be eliminated by defamation, extermination, prohibition of their writings, destruction of their synagogues, and exclusion into ghettos and despised occupations. During these 19 centuries, Judaism and Christianity never talked as equals. Disputation and polemics were the media of expression. More recent developments reflect the continuation of patterns of ethnic behaviour growing out of this heritage, by which Jews have been excluded by non-Jews, and have, in turn, themselves drawn together in separate communities.

No Christian can exempt himself from involvement in the guilt of Christendom. But Lutherans bear a special responsibility for this tragic history of persecution, because the Nazi movement found a climate of hatred already in existence. The kindness of Scandinavian Lutherans towards Jews cannot alter the ugly facts of forced labour and concentration camps in Hitler's Germany. That the Nazi period fostered a revival of Luther's own medieval hostility toward Jews, as expressed in pugnacious writings, is a special cause of regret. Those who study and admire Luther should acknowledge unequivocally that his anti-Jewish writings are beyond any defense.

In America, Lutherans have been late and lethargic in the struggle for minority rights in the face of inherited patterns of prejudice. We have also been characterized by an inadequate level of ethical sensitivity and action in social and political areas.

Distinctive ideas, doctrines, practices

Customarily, American Lutherans have increased misunderstanding by trying to picture Jews as a "denomination" or "faith-community" like themselves. Actually, Jewishness is both a religious phenomenon and a cultural phenomenon which is exceedingly hard to define. While for most Jews, ancient and modern, it is seen as a matter of physical descent, the aspects of religion and nationhood have at times occupied decisive positions, as is currently true in regard to Zionism. We create misunderstanding when we persist in speaking of "Jewish" creeds and "Jewish" theology, for not all Jews necessarily believe in Judaism, although that religion is their heritage.

Judaism, while it does indeed have teachings, differs markedly from Christian denominations in that its essence is best summed up not in a set of beliefs or creeds, but in a way of life. The distinctive characteristics of the words "Jew" and "Judaism" should neither be ignored nor should they be revised to fit better with Christian presuppositions. We must rather allow Jewishness to be defined by Jews, and content ourselves with the already tremendous difficulties of trying to keep aware of the complexities of this shifting and not uncontradictory self-understanding.

To the extent that both religious practices and theological reflection manifest themselves among Jews, some basic guidelines can be attempted. There is no reason why Jewish practices and beliefs should be understood or judged differently from those of any minority group. They ought, indeed, to be respected especially by Christians, since they flow from a tradition which served as the "mother" of Christianity. But even where they are in disagreement with the practices and beliefs of Christians, they still deserve the same full protection and support which are given to the religious convictions of any American citizen. While modern interest in ethnicity has furthered the appreciation of diversity of heritages, American Lutherans still need warnings against bigotry and urgings to work toward minority rights.

The unique situation of the sharing of the books of the Hebrew Scriptures by Lutherans and Jews is the source of great problems as well as the potential for significant dialogue. Because Jews are not a "denomination" with a unity shaped by a theological consensus, these Scriptures do not have the same role for them as they do for us. For both Jews and Lutherans the Old Testament has a kind of mediate authority. For Jews this authority is mediated by millenia of tradition and by the individual's choice as to whether or not he will be "religious". For Lutherans as well, the Hebrew Scriptures do not have independent authority. They gain their significance from their role as *Old* Testament and are subordinated to the New Testament Christ, in whom they find a complex fulfilment, involving cancellation as well as acceptance, and reinterpretation as well as reaffirmation. Lutherans must affirm what Jews are free to accept or reject, namely, that it is the same God who reveals himself in both Scriptures. The consequence of this is that Lutherans must view Judaism as a religion with which we in part agree wholeheartedly and yet in part disagree emphatically. Judaism worships the same God as we do (the God of Abraham is our God), yet it disavows the Christ in whom, according to Christian faith, all God's promises have their fulfilment and through whom God has revealed the fullness of his grace.

In view of these divergences, Lutherans and Jews will differ, sometimes drastically, about questions of biblical interpretation, especially in regard to Christian claims about the fulfilment of the Old Testament.

Such disagreements should not be the cause of either anger or despair, but rather should be seen as the doorway to a dialogue in which there can occur the discovery of both the real sources of the divergences and their appropriate degree of importance. Out of such learning there can come a mutuality of understanding which can make witness far more meaningful.

III. Respect and cooperation

In recognition of the solidarity that unites us and of the tensions and disagreements which have divided us, we affirm the desire of the American Lutheran Church to foster a relationship of respect and cooperation with our Jewish neighbours.

Cooperation in social concern

Jews and Lutherans live together in the same society. They have common problems and obligations. The bonds of common citizenship ought to impel Lutherans to take the initiative in promoting friendly relationships and in making common cause with Jews in matters of civic and social concern. It is of special importance that Lutherans demonstrate their commitment to the intrinsic worth of Jewish people by giving them all possible assistance in the struggle against prejudice, discrimination, and persecution. Jews and Lutherans need not share a common creed in order to cooperate to the fullest extent in fostering human rights.

A mutual sharing of faith

Within a context of respect and cooperation, Lutherans should invite Jews to engage in a mutual sharing of convictions. Lutherans who are aware of the Jewish roots of their faith will be moved by both a sense of indebtedness and a desire for deeper understanding to share on the level of religious commitment. Many Lutherans wish to engage in a mutual sharing of convictions, not only for the sake of greater maturity, but also because Christian faith is marked by the impulse to bear witness through word and deed to the grace of God in Jesus Christ.

It is unrealistic to expect that Lutherans will think alike or speak with one voice on the motive and method of bearing witness to their Jewish neighbours. Some Lutherans find in Scripture clear directives to bear missionary witness in which conversion is hoped for. Others hold that when Scripture speaks about the relation between Jews and Christians, its central theme is that God's promises to Israel have not been abrogated. The one approach desires to bring Jews into the body of Christ, while the other tends to see the church and the Jewish people as together forming the one people of God, separated from one another for the time being, yet with the promise that they will ultimately become one.

It would be too simple to apply the labels "mission" and "dialogue" to these points of view, although in practice some will want to bear explicit witness through individuals, special societies, or ecclesiastical channels, while others will want to explore the new possibilities of interfaith dialogue. Witness, whether it be called "mission" or "dialogue", includes a desire both to know and to be known more fully. Such witness is intended as a positive, not a negative act. When we speak of a mutual sharing of faith, we are not endorsing a religious syncretism. But we understand that when Lutherans and Jews speak to each other about matters of faith, there will be an exchange which calls for openness, honesty, and mutual respect. One cannot reveal one's faith to another without recognizing the real differences that exist and being willing to take the risk of confronting these differences.

We wish to stress the importance of interfaith dialogue as a rich opportunity for growth in mutual understanding and for a new grasp of our common potentiality for service to humanity. We commend to the American Lutheran Church the LCUSA document, "Some Observations and Guidelines for Conversations between Lutherans and Jews", as a helpful means toward realizing the goals of interfaith dialogue. It should be understood that the LCUSA document limits itself to the aims and methods of dialogue and does not attempt to cover the entire field of Lutheran-Jewish relationships. Consequently, its comment that "neither polemics nor conversions are the aim of such conversations" does not rule out mission.

The State of Israel

The LCUSA "Guidelines" wisely suggest that "the State of Israel" be one of the topics for Jewish-Lutheran conversations. The tragic encounter of two peoples in the Middle East places a heavy responsibility upon Lutherans to be concerned about the legitimacy of the Jewish state, the rights of the Palestinians, and the problems of all refugees.

The history and circumstances of the Israeli-Arab conflict are very complicated. It is understandable that Lutherans should be deeply divided in their evaluation of the situation in the Middle East. In Jewish opinion, Israel is more than another nation. It is a symbol of resurrection following upon the near extinction of the Jewish people within living memory. There are also some Lutherans who find a religious significance in the State of Israel, seeing in recent events a fulfilment of biblical promises.

Other Lutherans espouse not a "theology of the land", but a "theology of the poor", with special reference to the plight of the Palestinian refugees. Still other Lutherans endorse what might be called a "theology of human survival", believing that the validity of the State of Israel rests on juridical and moral grounds.

It seems clear that there is no consensus among Lutherans with respect to the relation between the "chosen people" and the territory comprising the present State of Israel. But there should be a consensus with respect to our obligation to appreciate, in a spirit of repentance for past misdeeds and silences, the factors which gave birth to the State of Israel and to give prayerful attention to the circumstances that bear on the search for Jewish and Arab security and dignity in the Middle East.

● From: *Luther, Lutherans and the Jewish people*, a study resource, 1974, pp.24-30.

Council of the
Evangelical Church in Germany

In May 1975 the Council of the Evangelical Church in Germany (Rat der Evangelischen Kirche in Deutschland) adopted an extensive study entitled "Christians and Jews" which had been worked out by a permanent study commission on "The Church and the Jewish People". It contains three parts: I. Common Roots; II. The Parting of the Ways; and III. Jews and Christians Today. Below are given part I and two chapters of Part III: chapter 2 on "The Two Modes of Jewish Existence", and chapter 3 on "The State of Israel".

I. Common roots

1. One God

When we Christians speak of God, we are of one mind with the Jews that the God to whom the Holy Scriptures bear witness, is One. Since the early period of Israel, it has been a fundamental principle that God as Creator and Redeemer lays claim to exclusiveness. It was in this that the Jews of the Old Testament era differed from other nations who recognized and worshipped several or even many gods. Witness to the One God was also a mark of Christians, and during the first centuries of Christian history Jews and Christians were equally maligned and persecuted for it.

The basic Jewish *credo* in our time as in those days, is: "Hear, O Israel, the Lord is our God, the Lord is One" (Deut. 6:4). Jesus and his disciples also pronounced these words as part of their daily prayer, as the Jews do even today. That same statement became the basis of the first article of the Christian confession of faith.

The link is also evident in the development of this confession by Jews and Christians. Faith in God the Creator is placed at the beginning of the Bible; it has pervaded Jewish prayer from its beginning and is a central article of Christian faith. Jews and Christians understand God as the God of all mankind while, at the same time, he has a particular relationship with those who belong to his people.

This relationship finds particular expression in man's faith in God, the Redeemer. The Old Testament attests to the experience of this faith in various ways: from the miraculous delivery of the people of Israel from Egyptian bondage to the expectation of the final return and redemption of the entire people. That theme was taken up by the New Testament and marked by a new experience: faith in the divine acts of Jesus' death and resurrection, the support of the Holy Spirit in the period between Easter and the Second Coming of Christ, and the expectation of redemption at the end of time. Hope in the resurrection of the dead, alluded to in the Old Testament, was further developed by Judaism at the time of Jesus. Since then, it has been an essential element of Jewish prayer language while in Christian expectations of the end of time, it is indissolubly joined to belief in the Resurrection of Jesus Christ.

Quite often elements characteristic of and basic to Christianity are also distinctive of Jewish piety. In Jewish prayers which for many centuries have been passed on from generation to generation, God the Creator and Redeemer who raises the dead, is addressed and praised as the merciful and compassionate one and Father of his own. Love for his people and for all men and assurance of the forgiveness of our sins are expressed in a variety of ways.

In Christian faith, these statements stand in the context of God's revelation in Christ. This is most clearly expressed in the One God who is confessed and invoked as the Father of Jesus Christ.

2. Holy Scripture

The first Christians, like all Jews, had a number of biblical books which basically correspond to what the Church later called the "Old Testament". These writings are in the New Testament called, "the Law and the Prophets" (Matt. 22:40). Frequently they are simply called the Scriptures since this collection was generally known and recognized as a fundamental testimony of faith. Christians as well as Jews derived abundant instruction from the Scriptures for everyday life, prayer, sermons and worship.

In proclaiming his message, Jesus quite naturally referred to the Scriptures as they were available to him. The dual command of love which He made the nucleus of his message, was derived from the Scriptures by connecting two originally separate statements: "You shall love the Lord your God with all your heart, and with all your soul, and with all your strength" (Deut. 6:5) and, "You shall love your neighbour as yourself" (Lev. 19:18). This was a permissible procedure within the framework of Jewish Scriptural interpretation of the time. Thus the learned Jew talking to Jesus agreed, "well answered, Master" (Mark 12:32). By applying this command to enemies, tax collectors, and Samaritans, Jesus drew consequences from it, though, that went beyond the Jewish interpretations.

Following Jesus, Paul made the Scriptures the basis for his proclamation and employed the rules common to Jewish interpretation at his time. It is noteworthy that Paul refers to words of Jesus in a few passages only while quoting the Scriptures very frequently. Yet, he also interprets the latter in a new way that is strange to Jews.

These Scriptures are common to Jews and Christians. They are made known to non-Jews in the Christian proclamation. Paul already addressed himself to Gentiles and, from that time on, non-Jews became familiar with the relationship of God with his people Israel and were taken into that history.

The Christian communities' own writings begin at an early stage. They refer constantly to the "Scriptures" while developing God's saving acts in Jesus Christ. These form the "New Testament" which Christians joined to the "Old Testament" to form their Bible.

Again and again in the course of her history, the church has struggled to comprehend the Old Testament. There also were repeated attempts to deprive individual books of their worth or deny recognition to the Old Testament as a whole, as part of Holy Scripture. Such attempts were rejected by the church, however, because she confesses the God of Abraham, Isaac, and Jacob as Father of Jesus Christ. Thus, the Old Testament, the Holy Scripture of the Jews, remains one of the two components of the Christian Bible.

3. The people of God

According to Old Testament belief, God is the Creator and Lord of the world as well as the God of his people Israel whom he chose and with whom he made a covenant. That is due, not to the virtues or merits of his people, but to a bestowal of the love of God.

Love of God for his people demands the people's love for their God which finds expression in doing his will. Israel, as a people, is to live according to the commandments revealed at Sinai. Even though the people as a whole may be found wanting in the required obedience, the Prophets proclaim that God holds to his election and calls his people to repentance so that they may completely fulfill his will.

This basic self-understanding as people of God is a determinant of Jews even of our day. This finds frequent expression in prayer where it says: "Thou has chosen us and has hallowed us among the nations." Though it is known that a large proportion of the people do not completely fulfill the commandments of God, Jewish tradition says: "All of Israel have a share in the coming world." The divine election remains valid for the sake of the covenant which God made with the fathers.

The New Testament, too, speaks of the people of God which, initially, refers to the people of Israel. Jesus says that He is sent to "the lost sheep of the house of Israel" (Matt. 15:24). And Paul confirms to the Jews that they are and will remain the people of God: "God has not rejected his people" (Rom. 11:2). He expects them to be included — either now or in the future — in the salvation revealed by Christ.

The barriers of belonging to a particular people are abolished in the Christian proclamation of the Gospels; all who believe in Jesus Christ are children of Abraham and heirs to the promise given to Israel. This is how the Church, the people of God from among the Jews and Gentiles, was born.

Together with the concept "people of God", the New Testament transfers basic elements of Old Testament covenantal thinking to the Christian community. The latter are called "a chosen race, a royal priesthood, a holy nation, God's own people" (1 Pet. 2:9), just as the Old Testament says of the people of Israel (Ex. 19:5-6).

Thus, Jews and Christians understand themselves as people of God. Despite their division, both are called and ordained to be witnesses of God in this world, to do his will, and to move towards the future fulfilment of his reign.

4. Worship

Jews and Christians gather for worship to hear the word of God, to confess their faith, and to pray. There are common elements in their worship which distinguish them from most other religions. These are based on the fact that both consider themselves bound by divine revelation to which the Holy Scriptures bear witness. Both cover all of the life of a devout person who, in faith and obedience to the word of God, should make all his life an expression of worship.

The present forms of Jewish worship are the result of a long development. In the course of this process, the Temple worship in Jerusalem with its offerings existed side by side with prayer services in synagogues, which could be held anywhere. After the destruction of the Temple in 70 AD, the synagogue service became the core of Jewish religious life. Christian worship, which had its origin in the celebration of the Lord's Supper, took over elements of the synagogue service and developed them independently.

Jewish and Christian worship, then, contain many similarities and hold many things in common, e.g. the weekly holiday (Sabbath/Sunday), the form of the word service (Scripture readings, prayers, blessings) with common liturgical expressions (Alleluyah, Amen), certain celebrations in the course of the year (Passover/Easter) and in the course of life (circumcision/baptism, affirmation of the hope for a future life at the burial of the dead). We must not overlook that existing differences were often created with the intent to separate one from the other.

Similarities in structure and form of the liturgical services permitted the first Christians to maintain their community with Jews by taking part in synagogue services. After a long period of separate development, reflections on the fellowship of Christians and Jews have led to attempts to worship together again, on certain occasions.

5. Justice and love

Christians and Jews are characterized in their self-understanding by the knowledge that they were chosen by God as partners to his covenant. In that election God reveals his love and his justice, from which grows the obligation for Jews and Christians alike, to work for a realization of justice and love in the world.

In all that God does, justice and love are one; that is why they should be one in man. Human justice must at all times be inspired by love, while human love depends on justice. Whether or not they are fulfilling this claim, greatly influences the credibility of Christians and Jews.

The Old Testament applies the commandment of love primarily to the people of God as partner in the Covenant. But it is also said of the stranger who lives with the people: "You shall love him as yourself" (Lev. 19:34).

Certain groups in post-biblical Judaism extended the commandment of love of neighbour still further, while Jesus did away with all limitations by calling for love of the enemy.

The requirement for life in justice, determined in all its particulars by obedience to the will of God, is strongly emphasized in Judaism. That could create the impression as if love were supplanted by justice. Yet, the Old Testament prophets as well as later teachers of Judaism justified such a life by the love of God for his people: out of love, God gave the Torah to his people. It comprises that sphere of life in which righteousness is realized in love of neighbour, as a response to that act of God.

In Christian understanding, too, justice and love belong together; but Christians consider God's act of justification in Jesus Christ a prerequisite for the realization of justice and love among men.

Thus, profound differences exist between Christians and Jews for the justification of love and justice; yet they hold much in common in the perception of concrete demands. For that reason, Christians and Jews can cooperate in the realization of justice and love in the world and in the service of peace.

6. *History and fulfilment*

In their relationship to history and its final goal, Jews and Christians are bound together by the experiences of the people of Israel in their history with God, ever since the time of Abraham.

Among the nations of that time, it was widely held that mankind and the world were at the mercy of fate in an eternal cycle of birth and death. The people of Israel, however, knew by experience — though often against their own ideas and wishes — that God was calling them on a way that knows no return. This road is leading towards a goal where Israel, together with the other nations, will receive final salvation in God.

Under the influence of such experiences, Jews and Christians believe that the process of history must not be seen as blind fate or a chain of erratic events. They realize and bear witness to the fact that the ultimate meaning and goal of history is God's salvation for all men.

Christians believe that in Jesus Christ the prophecies of God's covenant with his people have gained a new and wider dimension to bring the world closer to fulfilment. It is at this point that we find the strain underlying the division: for Jews it is the Torah that leads to fulfilment, while for Christians salvation lies in faith in the Messiah Jesus who has come already and in the expectation of his second coming.

Despite this, the many things held in common by Christians and Jews obligate them to endure that tension and to make it fruitful for the fulfilment of history, expected by both. Christians and Jews are called to carry out their responsibilities for the world, not against or independent of one another, but jointly under the will of God.

III. Jews and Christians today

2. *The two modes of Jewish existence*

Since earliest times, Jews have been living in the land of Israel as well as outside of it. Only a part of those deported into Babylonian exile, for instance, returned to the country. Later on, a Jewish diaspora developed in Syria, Egypt, and the whole Mediterranean area, by emigration and missionary work. At the time of Jesus, the diaspora was culturally important and numerically stronger than the Jewry within the country of Israel. In our time, too, the majority of Jews live outside the country.

Jewish faith, nevertheless, inseparably links the election of the people to the election of the land. The Book of Deuteronomy clearly says that only within the country can Israel be fully obedient to God. Her prophets promise the return of the people to the land, where the Torah can be fulfilled and God will establish his kingdom. Jews have always held fast to this bond between people and land. After the failure of the Jewish wars of liberation in the first and second century AD, Jewish life was at times very precarious and existed in certain parts of the country only, mainly in Galilee. At that time Jewish teachers demanded that the people remain in the country or return there. In their prayers Jews ask every day: "Unite us from the four corners of the earth." The liturgy of the first Passover night culminates in the exclamation: "Next year in Jerusalem." Many details of the Law as well as all festivals of the Jewish year are based on this link between people and land, so that in the traditional view Jewish existence can be fully lived only in the country of Israel.

That makes diaspora life a temporary situation which must be overcome and that is why diaspora Jews since the times of antiquity have again and again been trying to maintain contact with the land. An individual could achieve such contact by donations for those living in the country, by pilgrimages, or by return — if only to be buried there. Again and again, immigration by sizeable groups took place, often impelled by messianic movements. The Zionist settlement movement of the last one hundred years is but a link in this long chain of attempts to restore the unity of people and land.

Yet, diaspora life was not merely considered a fate to be endured, an inscrutable divine path, or a temptation to surrender through assimilation. There always existed individual Jews and Jewish groups who saw in the diaspora a chance for the Jewish people to make known among the nations the message of the One God. Religiously, ethically, and culturally, the Jewish disapora made considerable contributions to many nations. The origin and development of Christianity and Islam were largely stamped by continuous contact with the Jewish disapora, just as Jews received impulses by living among other nations and religions.

3. The State of Israel

Jewish settlement in the country and the situation after Auschwitz were the two decisive factors leading to the founding of the State.

Towards the end of the nineteenth century, traditional anti-Judaism among Christians developed into a new form of racist anti-semitism. In its final consequence, it culminated in the mass murder of European Jewry by the National Socialist state. Following this indescribable catastrophe, the major powers finally gave support and recognition to the demand for an independent state in Palestine. The founding of the state brought to a close the development that since the end of the nineteenth century had made the old land of Israel to an ever increasing degree a place of refuge for persecuted Jews.

It was not only the pressure of an inimical environment, though, that caused Jews to return to their land but the realization of a longing for Zion, sustained for millenia. Beyond its political function, then, the State of Israel has religious meaning for many Jews. They perceive of the Bible and post-biblical tradition in a completely new manner. More and more, Israel is becoming an intellectual centre that influences the diaspora. A basic Israeli law grants all Jews the privilege to live in the country and obtain citizens' rights, thereby endeavouring to guarantee the survival of diaspora Jews in case of renewed persecutions or threats to their identity.

Politically speaking Israel is a modern secular state, organized as a parliamentary democracy, just as in antiquity the Jewish people fashioned their state on contemporary models. Yet, such a characterization does not fully describe the modern State: its name and founding document expressly place it within the tradition of Judaism and, thereby, within the context of the chosen people's history. It is the task of the State of Israel to guarantee the existence of this people in the country of their forefathers. This implication has meaning for Christians as well. After all the injustice inflicted upon the Jews — particularly by Germans — Christians are obliged to recognize and support the internationally valid United Nations Resolution of 1948 which is intended to enable Jews to live a secure life in a state of their own.

At the same time, Christians must energetically work toward the proper settlement of justified claims by both sides, Arabs and Jews. Neither should the Palestinian Arabs alone have to bear the consequences of the conflict, nor should only Israel be held responsible for the situation. For that reason, even those not directly involved must participate in efforts to procure a durable peace in the Middle East. German Christians in particular must not evade their part in this task. They will also have to strengthen their bond with Arab Christians who by the conflict were placed in a very difficult situation.

● From: *Christen und Juden. Eine Studie des Rates der Evangelischen Kirche in Deutschland*, Gütersloh, Gütersloher Verlagshaus Gerd Mohn, 1975. English translation: Croner, *Stepping Stones to Further Jewish-Christian Relations*, London, Stimulus Books, 1977, pp.133-148.

Document 15

Central Board of the Swiss Protestant Church Federation

In May 1977 the Central Board of the Swiss Protestant Church Federation (Schweizerischer Evangelischer Kirchenbund) published "Reflections on the Problem 'Church-Israel'".

Foreword

The Central Board of the Schweizerischer Evangelischer Kirchenbund (Swiss Protestant Church Federation) is deeply interested in the destiny of the Jewish people as the Covenant People of God in the Old Testament, the people from whose ranks were descended Jesus of Nazareth, the early apostles and the oldest Christian community. The history of the church as well as the history of the Jews down to the present time questions us about the relationship of church and Israel and about the stand taken by Christians to Jews.

The ingathering of many Jews in parts of the Land promised them in the Old Testament causes the church in her thought and action to share with burning concern in the problems of the Near East in which Jews and Arabs confront each other.

Through these problems and through the religious-historical links with Judaism and also through the options made inside the church, which range from solidarity with the State of Israel, over theological dialogue, to a call for missions to the Jews, the Board is being asked questions which claim the attention of all Christians.

The Board therefore commissioned a working group consisting of Prof. Robert Martin-Achard of Geneva, Martin Klopfenstein of Bern and the president of the Council of Christians and Jews, Pastor Heinrich Oskar

Kuehner of Basle, in whose work Dr Walter Sigrist, president of the Federation, has also taken part. The texts submitted by this working group were discussed by the Board itself and are herewith offered to the public as "Reflections on the Problem Church-Israel" in order to stimulate personal thinking.

I. The people of God's covenant

"Has God rejected his people? By no means" (Rom. 1:11).

The people of the Old Testament of which present-day Judaism considers itself the heir, is still in existence and lives partly again in the Land of its Fathers — this in spite of its own aspirations at assimilation. This fact earnestly reminds the church of its duty to be concerned with this people. This duty, which is based upon what Paul calls "the mystery of Israel", is independent of the existence of the State, it confronts the church permanently.

We state the following points:

1. According to the witness of the Old and New Testaments God called the people of Israel to be his covenanted people. This election is but a free choice of grace, i.e. is not based upon any special quality which Israel might possess. The object of the election is to bear witness to the God of Abraham, Isaac and Jacob in the face of the world and to serve him. According to Gen. 12:3, God will thereby let his blessing come upon all nations. This alone constitutes the specific character of the people of Israel. There is no biological explanation for this specificity.

2. This covenant relationship should become manifest in the whole life of this people. This intention conforms to the will of God "to become flesh and dwell among us", and "to let his kingdom come to us", and "to let his will be done in heaven and on earth". This intention has finally become fully realized in Christ Jesus — a Jew.

3. Indeed the Jewish people all through its history has often broken the covenant and failed to fulfill God's will. Yet this does not annul God's fidelity to the covenant. Nor does the non-recognition of Jesus of Nazareth as the Christ by the majority of the Jews repeal the covenant promise given to the Jewish people according to Rom. 9-11.

4. Because God has not rejected his people, there is no question that the church has taken the place of Israel as "the new people of God". Although the church, already in the New Testament, applied to herself several promises made to the Jewish people she does not supersede the covenant

people, Israel. Rather, Israel and the church stand side by side and belong together in several ways, while being at the same time separate on essentials. It should be important for us, Christians, to recognize what links us to the Jews and what separates us from them. We are conscious that there are clearly different views on this point within the church.

II. Christians and Jews belong together

"The faith of Christ links us together"... (Shalom Ben Chorin).

1. Jesus was a Jew, "born of a Jewish mother". He was sent to the Jews first (Matt. 15:24). His message is of value for "the Jew first and then also for the Greek" (Rom. 1:16 and elsewhere in Rom.).

2. The teaching of Jesus is rooted in Jewish thinking, in Jewish teaching and in Jewish life.

3. The church has included the Old Testament in her canon. The New Testament cannot be fully understood without the help of the Old.

4. Historically the Christian church has grown out of Judaism. This existing relationship must be respected at all times.

5. The early Christians were Jews and understood themselves as members of the Jewish people who believed in Christ Jesus.

6. The Christian church has taken over many customs from Judaism, e.g. the celebration of the Seventh Day, Passover, Pentecost, the pattern of public worship with readings and prayers from the Bible, singing and praying in the words of the psalms etc.

III. Christians and Jews have been separated from one another

..."Faith in Jesus separates us..." (Shalom Ben Chorin).

1. The attitude to Jesus is the central point of parting between Judaism, and the church. This was manifest already in the New Testament and is so still today.

The rift has grown deeper through the following facts:
— that on the part of Christians, the crucifixion of Jesus is often ascribed to the Jews as a collective guilt;
— that on the part of Christians, the Jews are often blamed for choosing their own righteousness as the way to God instead of the grace of God.

2. Added to this comes the fact that in the eyes of the Jews it is unthinkable to belong to the people of God unless one observes their own religious prescriptions (e.g. circumcision, dietary laws, sabbath, etc.).

From the Jewish point of view the ill-treatment of Jews by Christians (cf. 3:1), their defamation and outlawing down to physical extermination over 1700 years have weighed heavily upon every attempt at a rapprochement on the part of Christians.

The silence of many churches on the persecutions of Jews in the twentieth century and on the threat to the State of Israel in our days has been a cause of bitter disillusionment for them.

3. The persecutions have caused theologians and lay people in Christian churches to rediscover the link between Judaism and Christianity, and led to a new understanding of their belonging together.

IV. Who are the Jews and who are the Christians?

We, Christians, have often had no idea at all of Judaism, or else a false one. It is an urgent task for Christian communities to correct our partial knowledge or ignorance of Judaism.

1. (a) This particularly concerns the proclamation of the gospel and the teaching of both young and adult. It is urgent to amend the wrong concept of the collective guilt of the Jews for the death of Jesus on the cross.

(b) The real cause of the separation of Jews and Christians in the first century should be correctly investigated.

(c) It is part of the programme of Christian communities to learn about Judaism through reading and personal contacts.

2. (a) Such efforts lead also to the self-knowledge of Christian churches. Many things which are commonly regarded as typically Christian (e.g. neighbourly love) are recognized as also typically Jewish, as taken over from Judaism and therefore as common good. On the other hand, what is really essential in the Christian faith will become clearer.

(b) The meeting with Judaism helps Christians better to understand Jesus and his message.

V. Mission also to the Jews?

1. "A church which is not missionary has resigned" *(demissioniert)* (Emil Brunner). Without a mission Christianity would have remained a sect within Judaism.

2. Mission means the proclamation of Jesus Christ, just as the Jews on their part have borne witness to us of the unity and holiness of God and still do so. Mission is not conversion to Christian culture and customs.

3. Christians have to bear witness of their faith in Christ also to the Jews. We regard the Jews as men whom "God so loved that he gave his only Son for them" (John 3:16).

4. The New Testament gives Christians unequivocal directions as to how they have to bear witness to their faith: "In your hearts reverence Christ as Lord! Always be prepared to make a defence to any one who calls you to account for the hope that is in you. Yet do it with gentleness and reverence" (1 Pet. 3:15-16a). We have also to consider that God alone can make converts, not we, men and women. This attitude as witnesses is also binding for Christians in their dialogue with Jews.

5. The phrase "mission to the Jews" puts Jews on a par with heathens and undervalues the specific position of the Jewish people among the nations (cf. 1:1), as well as the fact that Judaism has known the God of the Bible and believed in him long before the birth of the church.

6. The Christian witness cannot be exhausted by dialogue alone nor by proclamation of the Word. It is credible only if everyone, including the Jews, is convinced through deeds.

VI. Zionism — State of Israel

Zionism is a movement rooted in biblical as well as post-biblical traditions. The Jewish tradition has always included and still includes in various forms the hope that the Jewish people would return to the land of their fathers (e.g. festivals, prayers, worship, etc.). The hope of Zion has been handed down and remains alive in the Jewish people to the present day.

Ever since the second half of the nineteenth century the political movement founded by Theodor Herzl has been able to inspire the Jews because, among other things, his modern Zionism was related to the traditional Jewish self-awareness. It strove to obtain a legally established home in the land of the fathers in order to guarantee an existence worthy of men in their own state to the Jews who were again and again being threatened and persecuted. It was also intended to facilitate for the Jewish people the realization of their right to self-determination.

1. The outcome of this movement was the foundation of the State of Israel, decided upon by UNO in Resolution 181(II) on 29 November 1947, and proclaimed on 14 May 1948.

2. Some Christians and many Jews see in the foundation of the State of Israel the fulfilment of the biblical promises. Others, among both Christians and Jews, regard it merely as a political deed which like every historical change entails political and human problems. The appreciation and the preservation of the Jewish people should determine our reflections between two standpoints.

3. This new state has become a homeland not only for many victims of West European persecutions, but also for emigrants under the pressure of East European, North-African and Oriental states.

When considering these problems we must take into account all these root causes which have led to the formation of the State of Israel and its present situation.

4. As often happens in world history, in this political growth of the new state the good fortune of some has become the misfortune of others. Together with the anxiety for the Jewish people we feel painfully concerned for the Palestinian Arabs who live inside and outside Israel.

5. We are conscious that antisemitic elements of European politics past and present are partially responsible for the present situation and that extreme hate propaganda, terror and the cold calculation of the great powers threaten the life of the Jews in the State of Israel, while in spite of all the lot of Palestinian Arabs is not being improved.

6. We consider it the duty of the Christian churches and all Christians to intervene in defence of the right to existence of the Jewish people, which is especially linked with us (cf. 1:4; 2:1-6) and to stand by Israel in her growing isolation.

7. We regard it also as a duty for Christian churches and all Christians to intervene so that the right to live and the conditions of life of Palestinian Arabs be appreciated. In this connection we regard it as an urgent task to work out a clarification of the concept "Palestinian" and to examine their possibility of self-determination.

8. Above all it is our duty to break down hate, to keep ourselves from the influence of one-sided propaganda and to serve reconciliation and peace. We reject every form of anti-Judaism, but also every form of anti-Arab feeling.

VII. Jerusalem

1. Various Christians, including evangelicals, identify the historically and topographically located city of Jerusalem with "the new Jerusalem", described in Revelations 21, and "the heavenly Jerusalem" in so many songs.

2. Most Christians have a special feeling of belonging to Jerusalem because she is the city of the beginnings and the place of the great events of salvation.

3. According to the churches of the Reformation neither the fulfilment of the promise nor the reality of faith in the events of salvation are linked to geographically and historically located "holy places".

4. The Reformed churches also are longing for the dignified and respectful preservation of the places where the events of salvation took place.

5. We are conscious that Jerusalem represents a complex cultural, political, religious and emotional problem. At the same time we recognize that the Israeli government is making great efforts to deal fairly with this situation, although these efforts cannot lead to the satisfaction of all parties concerned.

We recommend:

a) that in Jerusalem today under Israeli administration the monuments connected with historical events are as much as possible maintained and kept in repair with respect and care;

b) that the Christian denominations as well as the Islamic and Jewish communities practise today their religions freely under Israeli administration and are able to fulfill their rites, as well as marriages, children's rights, burials and religious instruction, each according to their own religiously determined legislations;

c) that freedom of religion is granted more extensively today than in Mandate times and also better than under Jordanian rule. (In the latter phase of the Mandate the Israelis were barred access to the Western Wall. Under Jordanian rule Christians living in Israel could visit the Holy Sepulchre only on definite festivals; Jews were not permitted at all to go to the Western Wall; Muslims from the Gaza strip could not travel to Jerusalem.)

Conclusion

We consider that it is an urgent duty for the Christian church to pray for Israel, for her neighbours and for peace in the Near East as well as the whole world. This prayer of intercession however does not absolve us of the above-mentioned tasks. It renders them all the more binding.

● From: *Überlegungen zum Problem "Kirche-Israel"*, herausgegeben vom Vorstand des Schweizerischen Evangelischen Kirchenbundes, Mai, 1977. English translation: H. Croner ed., *More Stepping Stones to Jewish-Christian Relations*, New York, Paulist Press, 1985, pp.198-204.

Document 16

Norwegian Bishops' Conference

In November 1977 the (Lutheran) Norwegian bishops' conference passed a statement on "Our Attitude Towards the People and the State of Israel".

The Bishops' Conference of 1977 looks with deep unrest upon acts and statements of recent times directed against the Jewish people and the State of Israel.

Antisemitism is an old and worldwide phenomenon with many sources, and the Christian church is not without guilt in the fact that this attitude also has cast a dark shadow on our Western culture for centuries. But as during the second world war, the church again wants to ascertain unambiguously that all antisemitism is sin and must be combatted without any reservation.

The Bishops' Conference realizes that the political conflict in the Middle East is a complicated matter, and it has no wish to take a position without reservations in terms of either party. We regard it as an unrenounceable necessity, both that Israel must be ensured the right to survive as a state of its own, within safe and guaranteed borders, and that the Arab inhabitants in the area must be granted full rights to develop their distinctive character and traditions.

We must, however, seriously point to the danger represented by the series of actions which have happened in recent times and by the arguments they are based on. Slogans have changed, but antisemitism and persecution of Jews in all times have been caused by lack of understanding of the specific character of the Jewish people: their awareness of being an elected people with a God-given calling and a special connection with the "promised land". In recent times this awareness of a Jewish specific character has resulted in the Zionistic ideology which stands behind the Jewish national state. To characterize this Jewish self-understanding with the modern, very emotional slogan of "racism" reveals both a lack of historical and religious understanding, and intolerance.

Historically and theologically, the church has a very near relation to the Jewish people. There the Christian faith has its roots. The church has, therefore, special presuppositions to understand how the Jewish people is connected with the land of their fathers. At the same time, the church also has a responsibility for contributing to ensuring for the Jews, wherever they may be found, conditions for keeping their spiritual distinctiveness.

Within the church itself, there may be different ways to understand the promises of the prophets and the relation of those promises to the actual state of Israel of our days. But, on Christian presuppositions, there may only be *one* meaning concerning the right of the Jews to exist in faithfulness to their spiritual heritage, without being exposed to unsympathetic charges and agitations and to actions in accordance with that.

We want, therefore, to urge the people of Norway to show a clear and fearless attitude over against any form of antisemitism, including the aggressive anti-Zionism.

● From: *Om holdningen til Israel som folk og stat*, minutes of the Norwegian Bishops' Conference 1977, 9 (authorized translation).

Synod of the Evangelical Church of the Rhineland (FRG)

As a result of several years of reflection and consultation the Synod of the Evangelical Church in the Rhineland (West Germany) in January 1980 adopted a statement "Towards Renovation of the Relationship of Christians and Jews".

Towards renovation of the relationship of Christians and Jews

Thou bearest not the root, but the root thee (Rom. 11:18b).

1. According to its "Message to the Congregations concerning the Dialogue between Christians and Jews" (12 January 1978) the Synod of the Evangelical Church in the Rhineland accepts the historical necessity of attaining a new relationship of the church to the Jewish people.

2. The church is brought to this by four factors:

1) The recognition of Christian co-responsibility and guilt for the Holocaust — the defamation, persecution and murder of the Jews in the Third Reich.

2) The new biblical insights concerning the continuing significance of the Jewish people within the history of God (e.g. Rom. 9-11), which have been attained in connection with the struggle of the Confessing Church.

3) The insight that the continuing existence of the Jewish people, its return to the Land of Promise, and also the foundation of the state of Israel, are signs of the faithfulness of God towards his people (cf. the study "Christians and Jews" III, 2+3).

4) The readiness of Jews, in spite of the Holocaust, to (engage in) encounter, common study and cooperation.

3. The Synod welcomes the study "Christians and Jews" of the Council of the Evangelical Church in Germany (EKD) and the supplementary and more precise "Theses on the Renewal of the Relationship of Christians and Jews" of the Committee "Christians and Jews" of the Evangelical Church of the Rhineland.

The Synod receives both thankfully and recommends to all congregations that the study and the theses be made the starting point of an intensive work on Judaism and the foundation of a new consciousness of the relationship of the church to the Jewish people.

4. In consequence the Synod declares:

1) We confess with dismay the co-responsibility and guilt of German Christendom for the Holocaust (cf. Thesis I).

2) We confess thankfully the "Scriptures" (Luke 24:32+45; 1 Cor. 15:3f.), our Old Testament, to be the common foundation for the faith and work of Jews and Christians (cf. Thesis II).

3) We confess Jesus Christ the Jew, who as the Messiah of Israel is the Saviour of the world and binds the peoples of the world to the people of God (cf. Thesis III).

4) We believe the permanent election of the Jewish people as the people of God and realize that through Jesus Christ the church is taken into the covenant of God with his people (cf. Thesis IV).

5) We believe with the Jews that the unity of righteousness and love characterizes God's work of salvation in history. We believe with the Jews that righteousness and love are the commands of God for our whole life. As Christians we see both rooted and grounded in the work of God with Israel and in the work of God through Jesus Christ (cf. Thesis V).

(6) We believe that in their respective calling Jews and Christians are witnesses of God before the world and before each other. Therefore we are convinced that the church may not express its witness towards the Jewish people as it does its mission to the peoples of the world (cf. Thesis VI).

7) Therefore we declare:

Throughout centuries the word "new" has been used in biblical exegesis against the Jewish people: the new covenant was understood in contrast to the old covenant, the new people of God as replacement of the old people of God. This disrespect to the permanent election of the Jewish people and its condemnation to non-existence marked Christian theology, the preaching and work of the church again and again right to the present day. Thereby we have made ourselves guilty also of the physical elimination of the Jewish people.

Therefore, we want to perceive the unbreakable connection of the New Testament with the Old Testament in a new way, and learn to understand the relationship of the "old" and "new" from the standpoint of the promise: in the framework of the given promise, the fulfilled promise and the confirmed promise. "New" means therefore no replacement of the "old". Hence we deny that the people Israel has been rejected by God or that it has been superseded by the church.

8) As we repent and convert we begin to discover the common confession and witness of Christians and Jews:

We both confess and witness God as the creator of heaven and earth, and know that we live our everyday life in the world blessed by the same God by means of the blessing of Aaron.

We both confess and witness the common hope in a new heaven and a new earth and the spiritual power of this messianic hope for the witness and work of Christians and Jews for justice and peace in the world.

5. The Synod recommends to all district synods to appoint someone representative of the Synod responsible for Christian-Jewish dialogue.

The Synod commissions the leading board of the church to constitute anew a committee "Christians and Jews" and to invite Jews to work within this committee. It is to advise the church leadership in all questions concerning the relationship of the church and Jewry and to assist the congregations and church districts towards a deeper understanding of the new standpoint in the relationship of Jews and Christians.

The Synod commissions the leading body of the church to consider in what form the Evangelical Church of the Rhineland can undertake a special responsibility for the Christian settlement Nes Ammim in Israel, as other churches (e.g. in the Netherlands and in the German Federal Republic).

The Synod commissions the leading body of the church to see to it that in the church instruction, in the continuing education, and in the advanced education of the church the matter of "Christians and Jews" shall be appropriately paid attention to.

The Synod considers it desirable that a regular teaching post (lectureship) with the thematic "Theology, Philosophy and History of Judaism" shall be established in the Wuppertal Theological Seminary and the University of Wuppertal, and requests the church leadership to negotiate with these institutions to this end.

● From: *Zur Erneuerung des Verhältnisses von Christen und Juden. Handreichung der Evangelischen Kirche im Rheinland*, Düsseldorf, 1980. English translation: F. Littell, revised by RR.

Document 18

Texas Conference of Churches

In January 1982 the Texas Conference of Churches adopted a state-ment on "Dialogue: a Contemporary Alternative to Proselytization".

Preamble: a new awareness

From the very beginning God's Spirit has moved over the waters of creation, bringing order out of chaos, light out of darkness, life out of death.

It was indeed this same Spirit of God which inspired the ecumenical movement among the churches of Jesus Christ. In our time we have seen the effects of this movement. Today Christians of diverse traditions enjoy increased understanding among themselves because they have responded to this gift of God's Holy Spirit. Through dialogue we have eliminated much ignorance and prejudice. We share a common mission of witness and service to the world. We have rejected proselytism as unworthy of our relationship to each other.

There is little doubt that the Spirit of God is once again moving over the waters. From every direction there are reports of a new awareness, a new consciousness, a new understanding between Jews and Christians. In this statement we wish to respond to this newest movement of the Spirit of God and even claim it as our own.

The task of ecumenism is far from completed. The movement toward greater unity is still a task of the Christian churches. We believe, however, that today the interfaith movement is summoning us into a renewed relationship with the Jewish people.

The Spirit of God moves among us through the events of our day. The Holocaust, the systematic and deliberate killing of six million Jews by the Third Reich, is the most singular event of our time summoning the Christian churches to re-examine (and reform) their traditional understanding of Judaism and the Jewish people. Biblical scholars and theologians of both Jewish and Christian traditions are affording us new insights into our common origins. Vatican Council II in its 1965 document, "Nostra Aetate", encouraged and called for "mutual understanding and appreciation" between Christians and Jews (paragraph 4).

In issuing this statement, it is the hope of the Texas Conference of Churches to encourage and promote this latest movement of the Spirit of God in our times. This statement is intended as a basis of discussion between Christians and Jews. We hope, too, that it will lead us into a renewed relationship with the Jews, one characterized by both dialogue and shared witness to the world.

I. Judaism as a living faith

A. We acknowledge with both respect and reverence that Judaism is a living faith and that Israel's call and covenant are still valid and operative today. We reject the position that the covenant between the Jews and God was dissolved with the coming of Christ. Our conviction is grounded in the teaching of Paul in Romans, chapters 9-11, that God's gift and call are irrevocable.

B. The Jewish people today possess their own unique call and mission before God and their covenant. They are called to faithfulness in fulfilling the command to witness to the world of the holiness of God's Name (Ex. 3:15, 9:16).

II. Relationship between the two covenants

A. The Christian covenant grew out of and is an extension of the Hebrew covenant. We Christians cannot understand ourselves or our relationship to God without a thorough knowledge of Judaism. "Thou bearest not the root, but the root thee" (Rom. 11:18).

B. Jews and Christians share a common calling as God's covenanted people. While we differ as to the precise nature of the covenant, we share a common history and experience of God's redemptive presence in history. Both Jews and Christians are called to faithfulness to the covenant as they understand it.

C. We believe that the interfaith movement is one toward greater understanding and unity among all major religions of the world, especially among Judaism, Christianity and Islam. The kinship of Jews and

Christians, however, is unique because of the special relationship between the two covenants.

D. We confess thankfully the Scriptures of the Jewish people, the Old Testament of our Bible, to be the common foundation for the faith and work of Jews and Christians. By referring to the Hebrew Scriptures as the "Old Testament" it is not our intention to imply that these Scriptures are not timelessly new for both Jew and Christian today.

III. Dialogue, the road to understanding

A. In response to the movement of the Holy Spirit today, we believe that the desired and most appropriate posture between Christians and Jews today is one of dialogue.

B. Dialogue is the road to understanding between the two faiths and leads us to enlightenment and enrichment. We believe that dialogue will reduce misunderstanding and prejudice (on both sides).

C. In a dialogical relationship we dedicate ourselves to the observance of the following principles:

1. The strictest respect for religious liberty.

2. Respect for others as they define themselves in light of their own experience and tradition.

3. Avoidance of any conversionary intent or proselytism in the relationship. This does not exclude Jews and Christians from affirming to each other their respective beliefs and values.

4. An assumption of good will on both sides and a willingness to listen and learn from each other. -

IV. Witnesses before each other and to the world

A. In the face of the growing secularizing and profaning of human life today, we believe that in their calling Jews and Christians are always witnesses of God in the presence of the world and before each other.

B. We acknowledge the universal nature of the mission [1] of Christian

---

[1] This part of the statement is intended to acknowledge the universal scope of the mission of the Christian churches. The church must evangelize all nations, in keeping with the command of Christ. While acknowledging this, the statement then goes on to address the special relationship between Christians and Jews and how this special relationship calls for dialogue and shared witness, rather than "unwarranted proselytism".

It is of interest that Prof. Tomaso Federici, in a paper presented at a meeting in Venice of the Catholic-Jewish Liaison Committee, expressed the church's mission, in reference to the Jews, in these words: "... renewed examination of Paul's text (in Romans) allows the conclusion that the church's mission to Israel consists rather in living a Christian life in total fidelity to the one God and his revealed word."

churches, and the need to witness, [2] to all nations. However, because of our unique relationship to Jews and Judaism, we believe that a posture of dialogue and shared mission is the one appropriate to this singular relationship.

C. In particular, it is our belief that Jews and Christians share a common mission to work together in the accomplishment of these tasks:

1) the hallowing of God's Name in the world;
2) respect for the dignity and importance of the individual person as created in the image and likeness of God;
3) the active pursuit of justice and peace among and within the nations of the world;
4) to be a sign of hope in the future as promised by God.

D. In view of this shared mission, we eschew all forms of unwarranted proselytism [3] between Christians and Jews. In particular, we as Christian leaders reject the following:

1) anything which infringes upon or violates the right of every human person or community not to be subjected to external or internal constraints in religious matters;
2) ways of preaching the gospel which are not in harmony with the ways of God, who invites us to repond freely to his call and serve him in spirit and truth;
3) any kind of witness or preaching which in any way constitutes a physical, moral, psychological or cultural constraint on Jews;
4) every sort of judgment expressive of discrimination, contempt, or restriction against individual Jews or against their faith, worship or culture;

---

[2] The word "witness" is an important one in defining the desired relationship between Jews and Christians. The word itself can mean many things. In this statement we, as Christians, use the word to mean the permanent activity whereby the Christian or the Christian community proclaims God's actions in history and seeks to show how in Christ has come "the light that enlightens every man" (May 1970 report of the Joint Working Group between the Roman Catholic Church and the World Council of Churches). Witnessing in this sense can take three forms: a) the witness of a life lived in justice, love and peace; b) the witness of a more formal proclamation of God's Word to the world, to society (includes liturgical gatherings of the community); c) the witness of social action on behalf of justice.

This statement recommends that such witnessing by Christians be done with due consideration of the rights of human persons to religious liberty. It also recommends that, in view of the special relationship between Christians and Jews, a common or shared witness is most appropriate.

[3] "Unwarranted proselytism" is a deliberately chosen expression, which defines proselytism in its pejorative sense, i.e. zeal for converting others to faith which infringes upon the rights of human beings.

5) untrue and hateful forms of comparison which exalt the religion of Christianity by throwing discredit on the religion of Judaism;
6) actions which, on educational, social or other pretexts, aim to change the religious faith of Jews by offering more or less overt protection and legal, material, cultural, political and other advantages;
7) attempts to set up organization of any sort for the conversion of Jews.

V. Conclusion: a Messianic hope

Jews and Christians share a great common hope in a future and final coming of God's reign in the world, a messianic age. While we differ in our understanding of whether and to what extent that promised age arrived in the person of Jesus Christ, we stand on common ground in hoping that one day there will be "a new heaven and a new earth" (Revelation, Isaiah). We believe that God's Spirit is moving over the waters once again. This statement is offered by the Texas Conference of Churches with the hope that it will facilitate the coming of that great day of righteousness and peace.

• From: *Current Dialogue*, No. 3, spring 1982, pp.16-20.

Synod of the
Evangelical Church of Berlin (West)

As a result of the discussions raised by the statement of the Evangelical Church of the Rhineland in 1980 (Document 17), several other West German churches adopted similar statements, among them the Synod of the Evangelical Church in Berlin (West) which in May 1984 agreed on "Points for Orientation on 'Christians and Jews'".

I

On 27 April 1950 the Synod of the Evangelical Church in Germany at its session in Berlin-Weissensee passed a "Statement on the Guilt against Israel" in which, under the heading of Romans 11:32:
— it reaffirmed its belief "in the Lord and Saviour who as a person came from the people of Israel";
— confessed "to the Church which is joined together in one body of Jewish Christians and Gentile Christians and whose peace is Jesus Christ";
— and emphasized as a part of its belief "God's promise to be valid for his chosen people even after the crucifixion of Jesus Christ".
On the basis of these statements of belief and confession the members of the Synod expressed their indignation "at the outrage which has been perpetrated against the Jews by people of our nation" caused "by omission and silence before the God of mercy". They warned against all balancing of guilt and injustice, asked all Christians to reject any antisemitism and to resist it and called them "to encounter Jews and Jewish Christians in a brotherly spirit". They shaped their certainty of Israel's sharing the hope

of the gospel into a prayer to "the Lord of mercy that he may bring about the Day of Completion when we will be praising the triumph of Jesus Christ together with the saved Israel".

On 28 January 1960, the Provincial Synod of Berlin-Brandenburg, on the occasion of antisemitic riots, reaffirmed this statement explicitly and unanimously. The members of the Synod confessed that they had "only insufficiently fulfilled" the obligations contained in it and passed a number of conclusions including in particular the following new points:

— the appeal to work out the biblical recognition "that our salvation cannot be severed from Israel's election";

— the encouragement in preaching, joint work of congregational groups, and teaching to the youth, to struggle for the recognition of God's will for Israel;

— the request to parents and educators to break "with the widespread embarrassing silence in our country about our share of the responsibility for the fate of the Jews";

— the request to seek for an encounter with the surviving Jewish fellow citizens;

— the encouragement to bear witness to our own life out of forgiveness towards the Jewish brothers and sisters by changing our ways, "so that they can forgive as well",

— and the exhortation to pray "for God's peace with Israel", "for Israel's peace among the nations, at the borders of its state and in our midst".

Since then the work towards an improvement of the Christian-Jewish relations in the Protestant sector has been further stimulated and promoted, regionally and nationwide, by a number of studies and statements. In spite of these and other efforts it still has not got beyond its first beginnings. Till today the burden of the centuries-old enmity against the Jews, in the church and in the political arena, has not been overcome.

II

Out of the recognition of the fundamental importance of Christian-Jewish relations for the church's teaching and life, in readoption of the above-mentioned documents, and in the awareness of the permanent latent or acute danger of attitudes and expressions of enmity against the Jews, the Synod of the Evangelical Church in Berlin-Brandenburg (Berlin West) on 20 May 1984 affirmed:

1. Our relations to the Jewish people are still overshadowed by the centuries-old attitude of enmity against the Jews in church and society, as well as by the persecution and murder of the Jews in the years 1933-45 in Germany and in the occupied territories. All the following generations have to face this guilt, even if no personal guilt for events before their life-time is to be attributed to them. The Holocaust remains a part of the history of our nation and of our church. Particularly in the Christian community whose members are closely linked to each other through the ages, the question of dealing with this guilt is of crucial relevance. Therefore, with our witness to the truth we oppose any denial and playing down of the Holocaust. After all that happened, the teaching, the education and the life of the church even more has to be shaped in a way that the history of guilt will not find a continuation, but that conversion and a new attitude will become possible.

2. Our relations to the Jewish people are determined by the common heritage of the Old Testament or Tenach and by the search for its adequate interpretation. This heritage constitutes the firm common ground for Jews and Christians. The Old Testament (Tenach) tells about the life with the God of the patriarchs and bears witness to this God's promise for Israel and the nations. Thus it joins the Christian community and the Jewish people together by the common hope in the victory of God's rule. Therefore, the Old Testament has to be read and heard more intensely as a witness which the Christian community shares with the people of Israel. In it the Christian community meets the God of the patriarchs as the father of Jesus Christ, as well as Israel as the people of God.

3. Our relations to the Jewish people are determined by the parting of the ways of Christians and Jews, already in early times. The mutual estrangement has obscured in many respects the view of the living unique character of the other. Therefore, endeavours have to be strengthened to approach with understanding, in service, teaching and education, the teaching and the life of the Jewish people in history and in the present and to describe them on their own terms.

4. Our relations to the Jewish people are characterized by the conviction of the Christian community that Jesus Christ has commissioned her with the witness of the gospel for Israel and for the nations in respectively different ways. Israel knows herself to be commissioned by God as well with the witness to all nations (Isa. 43:10). Admittedly, the church's witness to the Jewish people has been distorted in history because Christians, against the gospel, did not live it as a witness of love.

Therefore, to bear witness to the Jewish people today means first of all to live a Christian life that makes discernible God's Yes to the permanent election of Israel; thus the community of Jesus Christ can prove to be the one that is reconciled with the God who has elected Israel.

5. Our relations to the Jewish people are often influenced by the anxiety that an understanding approach to its life, its history and its tradition might endanger the Christian identity. Opposite to such an anxiety, however, stands the experience that meeting and understanding biblical Jewish life rather enriches the Christian faith instead of curbing it. Listening to and learning of Jewish traditions of faith, to which Jewish Christians substantially can contribute, therefore offers a chance to comprehend the Christian faith itself in a deeper and richer way.

6. Our relations to the Jewish people are also to be seen against the background of the establishment and the existence of the State of Israel in our days. Our affirmative stand towards the existence of this state is connected with the concern for a peaceful solution in the Near East which also includes the rights of the Palestinian Arabs and the Christians among them. Only as far as the specific circumstances of the emergence of the State of Israel, the differentiation of the Israeli society and the difficulties of a judgment from the outside are kept in consideration, discussions in Christian circles could be of any help for the forming of political opinions among the people concerned in Israel and in the Near East.

7. Our relations to the Jewish people are characterized by the fact that in Germany, after the persecution and the murder of the Jews during the years of 1933-45, there are only a few and small Jewish congregations. Therefore, even more is it part of the task of the church to search for the contact with the Jewish congregations and to promote encounters between Christians and Jews in this country and in Israel.

III

For the reasons named the Synod confirms its intention to support the activities of those Berlin church institutions and groups which — as e.g. the Evangelical Academy, the Working Group on Christians and Jews, the Permanent Committee of Jews and Christians, the Institute for Catechetic Service, and the Institute on the Church and Jewish People at the Kirchliche Hochschule Berlin — particularly work for an improvement of Christian-Jewish relations.

It asks the Berlin Missionswerk to report to all concerned on the discussions about these questions in and with the partner churches in the Near East.

It asks the congregations to make use of the opportunities existing with these institutions and to make the work for better relations with the Jewish people, according to the spirit of the points explained, one of their permanent tasks.

It asks the future Synod to make the continuation of the work on the issue "Christians and Jews" on the synod level its own concern, if necessary, to set up a working group, and to make available working material to the congregations.

It asks the various institutions concerned with tasks of education to give the issue of the renovation of the Christian-Jewish relations a firm place in teaching and education.

It asks the ministers to use more frequently Old Testament texts in service and education, and in this connection to give expression to the permanent election of Israel and to the permanent solidarity of Christians and Jews.

● From: *Berliner Theologische Zeitschrift. Theologia Viatorum Neue Folge*, 1, 1984, pp.368-371. English translation: RR.

General Assembly
of the Presbyterian Church (USA)

As a "product of a project begun in 1981" the General Assembly of the Presbyterian Church (USA) in June 1987 adopted a statement on "A Theological Understanding of the Relationship between Christians and Jews".

Purpose

Christians and Jews live side by side in our pluralistic American society. We engage one another not only in personal and social ways but also at deeper levels where ultimate values are expressed and where a theological understanding of our relationship is required. The confessional documents of the Reformed tradition are largely silent on this matter. Hence this paper has been prepared by the church, as a pastoral and teaching document, to provide a basis for continuing discussion within the Presbyterian community in the United States and to offer guidance for the occasions in which Presbyterians and Jews converse, cooperate and enter into dialogue. What is the relationship which God intends between Christians and Jews, between Christianity and Judaism? A theological understanding of this relationship is the subject which this paper addresses.

Context

Theology is never done in a vacuum. It influences and is influenced by its context. We do our theological work today in an increasingly global and pluralistic context — one that is interpersonal and intercommunal as well. Moreover, as Presbyterians we do our theological work on the basis of Scripture, in the context of our faith in the living presence of Jesus

Christ through the Holy Spirit, and of the church's theological tradition. A few words about each of these dimensions of our context may be helpful in understanding this paper.

The context in which the church now witnesses is more and more global and pluralistic. Churches have been planted in every nation on earth, but in most places Christians exist as a minority. The age of "Christendom" has passed, and the age of an interdependent global society is fast emerging. Things said by Christians in North America about the relationships of Christians and Jews will be heard by Christians in the Middle East, where there are painful conflicts affecting the entire region. Moreover it is increasingly difficult to ignore the existence of other religious communities and non-religious movements in the world, many of which challenge our truth claims. What we say on the subject before us will be considered by these as well. We must be sensitive as we speak of the truth we know, lest we add to the suffering of others or increase hostility and misunderstanding by what we say.

The context in which the church now witnesses is also interpersonal and intercommunal. The reality of which we speak consists of individual persons and of entire peoples who carry within themselves real fears, pains and hopes. Whatever the Presbyterian Church (USA) says about the relationship of Christians and Jews must be appropriate to our North American setting, and yet sensitive to the deep longings and fears of those who struggle with this issue in different settings, especially in the Middle East. Recent General Assemblies of the Presbyterian Church (USA) have maintained a clear and consistent position concerning the struggle in the Middle East as a matter of the church's social policy. The General Assembly regards the theological affirmations of the present study as consistent with the church's prior policy statements concerning the Middle East, which speak of the right of statehood in Palestine for Palestinians (c.f. Minutes of the 198th General Assembly (1986), PC(USA), Part I, p.86) and the right of the State of Israel to exist within secure borders established by the United Nations General Assembly resolutions. Therefore, the attention of the church is again called to the church's policy enunciated in 1974, reaffirmed in 1984, which reads in part:

> The right and power of Palestinian people to self-determination by political expression, based upon full civil liberties for all, should be recognized by the parties in the Middle East and by the international community... The Palestinian people should be full participants in negotiations... through representatives of their own choosing.

The right and power of Jewish people to self-determination by political expression in (the State of) Israel, based upon full civil liberties for all, should be recognized by the parties in the Middle East and by the international community (c.f. Minutes of the 196th General Assembly (1984), PC(USA), Part I, p.338; see also pp.335-339, "Resolution on Middle East", p.82, GA Amendments to Resolution).

The context of the church's witness includes also the fact that our church is deeply bound to its own heritage of Scripture and theological tradition. In discussing the relationship of Christians and Jews, we cannot separate ourselves from the Word of God, given in covenant to the Jewish people, made flesh in Jesus Christ, and ever renewed in the work of the Holy Spirit among us. Acknowledging the guidance of the church's confessional tradition, we recognize our responsibility to interpret the Word for our situation today. What the Presbyterian Church (USA) says on this complex subject will ultimately be evaluated in terms of the theological contribution that it makes.

The context of the church's witness includes, finally and most basically, the real presence of the risen Lord. We make our declarations within the love of Jesus Christ who calls us to witness, serve and believe in his name. Since our life is a part of what we say, we seek to testify by our deeds and words to the all-encompassing love of Christ through whom we "who were far off have been brought near" to the covenants of promise.

Background

This theological study is not unprecedented. Since World War II, statements and study documents dealing with Jewish-Christian relations have been issued by a number of churches and Christian bodies. Among these are the Vatican's "Nostra Aetate" (1965), the report of the Faith and Order Commission of the World Council of Churches (1968), the statement of the Synod of the Netherlands Reformed Church (1970), the statement of the French Bishops' Committee for Relations with the Jews (1973), the report of the Lutheran World Federation (1975), the statement of the Synod of the Evangelical Church of the Rhineland in West Germany (1980), the report of the Christian/Jewish Consultation Group of the Church of Scotland (1985), and the study of the World Alliance of Reformed Churches (1986).

The present study has been six years in preparation. It is the product of a project begun in 1981 within the former Presbyterian Church, US, then redeveloped and greatly expanded in scope and participation in 1983 upon the reunion which brought into being the Presbyterian Church (USA). The study has been developed under the direction of the church's Council on Theology and Culture, through a process which involved many people reflecting diverse interests and backgrounds, both in the United States and the Middle East.

In the course of addressing this subject, our church has come to see many things in a new light. The study has helped us to feel the pain of our Jewish neighbours who remember that the Holocaust was carried out in the heart of "Christian Europe" by persons many of whom were baptized Christians. We have come to understand in a new way how our witness to the gospel can be perceived by Jews as an attempt to erode and ultimately to destroy their own communities. Similarly, we have been made sensitive to the difficult role of our Arab Christian brothers and sisters in the Middle East. We have listened to the anguish of the Palestinians, and we have heard their cry.

The paper which we here present to the church does not attempt to address every problem, nor to say more than we believe that we are able truly to say. It consists of seven theological affirmations, with a brief explication of each. Together they seek to lay the foundation for a new and better relationship under God between Christians and Jews. They are:

1) a reaffirmation that the God who addresses both Christians and Jews is the same — the living and true God;
2) a new understanding by the church that its own identity is intimately related to the continuing identity of the Jewish people;
3) a willingness to ponder with Jews the mystery of God's election of both Jews and Christians to be a light to the nations;
4) an acknowledgment by Christians that Jews are in covenant relationship with God, and the consideration of the implications of this reality for evangelism and witness;
5) a determination by Christians to put an end to "the teaching of contempt" for the Jews;
6) a willingness to investigate the continuing significance of the promise of "land", its associated obligations, and to explore the implications for Christian theology;
7) a readiness to act on the hope which we share with the Jews in God's promise of the peaceable kingdom.

These seven theological affirmations with their explications are offered to the church not to end debate but to inform it, and thus to serve as a basis for an ever deepening understanding of the mystery of God's saving work in the world.

Definitions and language

The defining of terms on this subject is complex, but unavoidable. We understand "Judaism" to be the religion of the Jews. It is practised by many today and extends back into the period of the Hebrew scriptures. Judaism of late antiquity gave rise to that form of Judaism which has been developing since the first century known as "Rabbinic Judaism". It gave rise to early Christianity as well. Both Christianity and Judaism claim relationship with the ancient people Israel; the use of the term "Israel" in this study is restricted to its ancient reference. When referring to the contemporary State of Israel this document will use "State of Israel".

We understand "Jews" to include those persons whose self-understanding is that they are descended from Abraham, Isaac and Jacob, and Sarah, Rebekah, Rachel, and Leah, and those converted into the Jewish community. We recognize that Jews are varied in the observance of their religion, and that there are many Jews who do not practise Judaism at all.

The language of this paper is conformable to General Assembly guidelines for inclusiveness within the Presbyterian Church (USA). It avoids gender-specific references either to God or to the people of God, except in reference to the Trinity and the Kingdom of God, and in direct quotation from Scripture. The word "Lord" is used only with reference to Jesus Christ. The paper acknowledges the role of both women and men in the church's tradition.

The following affirmations are offered to the church for our common edification and growth in obedience and faith. To God alone be the glory.

Affirmations and explications

1. We affirm that the living God whom Christians worship is the same God who is worshipped and served by Jews. We bear witness that the God revealed in Jesus, a Jew, to be the Triune Lord of all, is the same one disclosed in the life and worship of Israel.

Explication

Christianity began in the context of Jewish faith and life. Jesus was a Jew, as were his earliest followers. Paul, the apostle of the Gentiles, referred to himself as a "Hebrew of the Hebrews". The life and liturgy of the Jews provided the language and thought forms through which the revelation in Jesus was first received and expressed. Jewish liturgical forms were decisive for the worship of the early church, and are influential still, especially in churches of the Reformed tradition.

Yet the relationship of Christians to Jews is more than one of common history and ideas. The relationship is significant for our faith because Christians confess that the God of Abraham and Sarah, and their descendants, is the very One whom the apostles addressed as "the God and Father of our Lord Jesus Christ". The one God elected and entered into covenant with Israel to reveal the divine will and point to a future salvation in which all people will live in peace and righteousness. This expectation of the reign of God in a Messianic Age was described by the Hebrew prophets in different ways. The Scriptures speak of the expectation of a deliverer king anointed by God, of the appearing of a righteous teacher, of a suffering servant, or of a people enabled through God's grace to establish the Messianic Age. Early Christian preaching proclaimed that Jesus had become Messiah and Lord, God's anointed who has inaugurated the kingdom of peace and righteousness through his life, death and resurrection. While some Jews accepted this message, the majority did not, choosing to adhere to the biblical revelation as interpreted by their teachers, and continuing to await the fulfilment of the messianic promises given through the prophets, priests and kings of Israel.

Thus the bond between the community of Jews and those who came to be called Christians was broken, and both have continued as vital but separate communities through the centuries. Nonetheless, there are ties which remain between Christians and Jews: the faith of both in the one God whose loving and just will is for the redemption of all humankind; and the Jewishness of Jesus whom we confess to be the Christ of God.

In confessing Jesus as the Word of God incarnate, Christians are not rejecting the concrete existence of Jesus who lived by the faith of Israel. Rather, we are affirming the unique way in which Jesus, a Jew, is the being and power of God for the redemption of the world. In him, God is disclosed to be the Triune One who creates and reconciles all things. This is the way in which Christians affirm the reality of the one God who is sovereign over all.

2. We affirm that the church, elected in Jesus Christ, has been engrafted into the people of God established by the covenant with Abraham, Isaac and Jacob. Therefore, Christians have not replaced Jews.

Explication

The church, especially in the Reformed tradition, understands itself to be in covenant with God through its election in Jesus Christ. Because the church affirms this covenant as fundamental to its existence, it has generally not sought nor felt any need to offer any positive interpretation of God's relationship with the Jews, lineal descendants of Abraham, Isaac and Jacob, and Sarah, Rebekah, Rachel and Leah with whom God covenanted long ago. The emphasis has fallen on the new covenant established in Christ and the creation of the church.

Some time during the second century of the Common Era a view called "supersessionism", based on the reading of some biblical texts and nurtured in controversy, began to take shape. By the beginning of the third century this teaching that the Christian church had superseded the Jews as God's chosen people became the orthodox understanding of God's relationship to the church. Such a view influenced the church's understanding of God's relationship with the Jews, and allowed the church to regard Jews in an inferior light.

Supersessionism maintains that because the Jews refused to receive Jesus as Messiah, they were cursed by God, are no longer in covenant with God, and that the church alone is the "true Israel" or the "spiritual Israel". When Jews continue to assert, as they do, that they are the covenant people of God, they are looked upon by many Christians as impertinent intruders, claiming a right which is no longer theirs. The long and dolorous history of Christian imperialism, in which the church often justified anti-Jewish acts and attitudes in the name of Jesus, finds its theological base in this teaching.

We believe and testify that this theory of supersessionism or replacement is harmful and in need of reconsideration as the church seeks to proclaim God's saving activity with humankind. The scriptural and theological bases for this view are clear enough; but we are prompted to look again at our tradition by events in our own time, and by an increasing number of theologians and biblical scholars who are calling for such a reappraisal. The pride and prejudice which have been justified by reference to this doctrine of replacement themselves seem reason enough for taking a hard look at this position.

For us, the teaching that the church has been engrafted by God's grace into the people of God finds as much support in Scripture as the view of supersessionism, and is much more consistent with our Reformed understanding of the work of God in Jesus Christ. The emphasis is on the continuity and trustworthiness of God's commitments and God's grace. The issue for the early church concerned the inclusion of the Gentiles in God's saving work, not the exclusion of the Jews. Paul insists that God is God of both Jews and Gentiles and justifies God's redemption of both on the basis of faith (Rom. 3:29-30). God's covenants are not broken. "God has not rejected his people whom he foreknew" (Rom. 11:2). The church has not "replaced" the Jewish people. Quite the contrary! The church, being made up primarily of those who were once aliens and strangers to the covenants of promise, has been engrafted into the people of God by the covenant with Abraham (Rom. 11:17-18).

The continued existence of the Jewish people and of the church as communities elected by God is, as the apostle Paul expressed it, a "mystery" (Rom. 11:25). We do not claim to fathom this mystery, but we cannot ignore it. At the same time we can never forget that we stand in a covenant established by Jesus Christ (Heb. 8) and that faithfulness to that covenant requires us to call all women and men to faith in Jesus Christ. We ponder the work of God, including the wonder of Christ's atoning work for us.

3. We affirm that both the church and the Jewish people are elected by God for witness to the world, and that the relationship of the church to contemporary Jews is based on that gracious and irrevocable election of both.

Explication

God chose a particular people, Israel, as a sign and foretaste of God's grace toward all people. It is for the sake of God's redemption of the world that Israel was elected. The promises of God, made to Abraham and Sarah and to their offspring after them, were given so that blessing might come upon "all families of the earth" (Gen. 12:1-3). God continues that purpose through Christians and Jews. The church, like the Jews, is called to be a light to the nations (Acts 13:47). God's purpose embraces the whole creation.

In the electing of peoples, God takes the initiative. Election does not manifest human achievement but divine grace. Neither Jews nor Christians can claim to deserve this favour. Election is the way in which God creates freedom through the Holy Spirit for a people to be for God and for others. God, who is ever faithful to the word which has been spoken, does not take back the divine election. Whenever either the Jews or the church have rejected God's ways, God has judged but not rejected them. This is a sign of God's redeeming faithfulness toward the world.

Both Christians and Jews are elected to service for the life of the world. Despite profound theological differences separating Christians and Jews, we believe that God has bound us together in a unique relationship for the sake of God's love for the world. We testify to this election, but we cannot explain it. It is part of the purpose of God for the whole creation. Thus there is much common ground where Christians and Jews can and should act together.

4. We affirm that the reign of God is attested both by the continuing existence of the Jewish people and by the church's proclamation of the Gospel of Jesus Christ. Hence, when speaking with Jews about matters of faith, we must always acknowlege that Jews are already in a covenantal relationship with God.

Explication

God, who acts in human history by the Word and Spirit, is not left without visible witnesses on the earth. God's sovereign and saving reign in the world is signified both by the continuing existence of, and faithfulness within, the Jewish people who, by all human reckoning, might be expected to have long since passed from the stage of history, and by the life and witness of the church.

As the cross of Jesus has always been a stumbling block to Jews, so also the continued existence and faithfulness of the Jews is often a stumbling block to Christians. Our persuasion of the truth of God in Jesus Christ has sometimes led Christians to conclude that Judaism should no longer exist, now that Christ has come, and that all Jews ought properly to become baptized members of the church. Over the centuries, many afflictions have been visited on the Jews by Christians holding this belief — not least in our own time. We believe that the time has come for Christians to stop and take a new look at the Jewish people and at the relationship which God wills between Christian and Jew.

Such reappraisal cannot avoid the issue of evangelism. For Jews this is a very sensitive issue. Proselytism by Christians seeking to persuade, even convert, Jews often implies a negative judgment on Jewish faith. Jewish reluctance to accept Christian claims is all the more understandable when it is realized that conversion is often seen by them as a threat to Jewish survival. Many Jews who unite with the church sever their bonds with their people. On the other hand, Christians are commissioned to witness to the whole world about the good news of Christ's atoning work for both Jew and Gentile. Difficulty arises when we acknowledge that the same Scripture which proclaims that atonement and which Christians claim as God's word clearly states that Jews are already in a covenant relationship with God who makes and keeps covenants.

For Christians, there is no easy answer to this matter. Faithful interpretation of the biblical record indicates that there are elements of God's covenant with Abraham that are unilateral and unconditional. However, there are also elements of the covenant which appear to predicate benefits upon faithfulness (see Gen. 17:1ff.). Christians, historically, have proclaimed that true obedience is impossible for a sinful humanity and thus have been impelled to witness to the atoning work of Jesus of Nazareth, the promised Messiah, as the way to a right relationship with God. However, to the present day, many Jews have been unwilling to accept the Christian claim and have continued faithfully in their covenant tradition. In light of scripture which testifies to God's repeated offer of forgiveness to Israel, we do not presume to judge in God's place. Our commission is to witness to the saving work of Jesus Christ; to preach good news among all the "nations" *(ethne)*.

Dialogue is the appropriate form of faithful conversation between Christians and Jews. Dialogue is not a cover for proselytism. Rather, as trust is established, not only questions and concerns can be shared but faith and commitments as well. Christians have no reason to be reluctant in sharing the good news of their faith with anyone. However, a militancy that seeks to impose one's own point of view on another is not only inappropriate but also counterproductive. In dialogue, partners are able to define their faith in their own terms, avoiding caricatures of one another, and are thus better able to obey the commandment, "Thou shalt not bear false witness against thy neighbour". Dialogue, especially in light of our shared history, should be entered into with a spirit of humility and a commitment to reconciliation. Such dialogue can be a witness that seeks also to heal that which has been broken. It is out of a mutual willingness to listen and to learn that faith deepens and a new and better relationship between Christians and Jews is enabled to grow.

5. We acknowledge in repentance the church's long and deep complicity in the proliferation of anti-Jewish attitudes and actions through its "teaching of contempt" for the Jews. Such teaching we now repudiate, together with the acts and attitudes which it generates.

Explication

Anti-Jewish sentiment and action by Christians began in New Testament times. The struggle between Christians and Jews in the first century of the Christian movement was often bitter and marked by mutual violence. The depth of hostility left its mark on early Christian and Jewish literature, including portions of the New Testament.

In subsequent centuries, after the occasions for the original hostility had long since passed, the church misused portions of the New Testament as proof texts to justify a heightened animosity toward Jews. For many centuries, it was the church's teaching to label Jews as "Christ-killers" and a "deicide race". This is known as the "teaching of contempt". Persecution of Jews was at times officially sanctioned, and at other times indirectly encouraged or at least tolerated. Holy Week became a time of terror for Jews.

To this day, the church's worship, preaching and teaching often lend themselves, at times unwittingly, to a perpetuation of the "teaching of contempt". For example, the public reading of Scripture without explicating potentially misleading passages concerning "the Jews", preaching which uses Judaism as a negative example in order to commend Christianity, public prayer which assumes that only the prayers of Christians are pleasing to God, teaching in the church school which reiterates stereotypes and non-historical ideas about the Pharisees and Jewish leadership — all of these contribute, however subtly, to a continuation of the church's "teaching of contempt".

It is painful to realize how the teaching of the church has led individuals and groups to behaviour that has tragic consequences. It is agonizing to discover that the church's "teaching of contempt" was a major ingredient that made possible the monstrous policy of annihilation of Jews by Nazi Germany. It is disturbing to have to admit that the churches of the West did little to challenge the policies of their governments, even in the face of the growing certainty that the Holocaust was taking place. Though many Christians in Europe acted heroically to shelter Jews, the record reveals that most churches as well as governments, the world over, largely ignored the pleas for sanctuary for Jews.

As the very embodiment of anti-Jewish attitudes and actions, the Holocaust is a sober reminder that such horrors are actually possible in this world, and that they begin with apparently small acts of disdain or expedience. Hence we pledge to be alert for all such acts of denigration from now on, so that they may be resisted. We also pledge resistance to any such actions, perpetrated by anyone, anywhere.

The church's attitudes must be reviewed and changed as necessary, so that they never again fuel the fires of hatred. We must be willing to admit our church's complicity in wrongdoing in the past, even as we try to establish a new basis of trust and communication with Jews. We pledge, God helping us, never again to participate in, to contribute to, or to allow the persecution or denigration of Jews, or the belittling of Judaism.

6. We affirm the continuity of God's promise of land along with the obligations of that promise to the people Israel.

Explication

As the Church of Scotland's (1985) report says:

> We are aware that in dealing with this matter we are entering a minefield of complexities across which is strung a barbed-wire entanglement of issues, theological, political and humanitarian.

However, a faithful explication of biblical material relating to the covenant with Abraham cannot avoid the reality of the promise of land. The question with which we must wrestle is how this promise is to be understood in the light of the existence of the modern political State of Israel which has taken its place among the nations of the world.

The Genesis record indicates that "the land of your sojournings" was promised to Abraham and his and Sarah's descendants. This promise, however, included the demand that "You shall keep my covenant..." (Gen. 17:7-8). The implication is that the blessings of the promise were dependent upon fulfilment of covenant relationships. Disobedience could bring the loss of land, even while God's promise was not revoked. God's promises are always kept, but in God's own way and time.

The establishment of the State of Israel in our day has been seen by many devout Jews as the fulfilment of God's divine promise. Other Jews are equally sure that it is not, and regard the State of Israel as an unauthorized attempt to flee divinely imposed exile. Still other Jews interpret the State of Israel in purely secular terms. Christian opinion is equally diverse. As Reformed Christians, however, we believe that no government at any time can ever be the full expression of God's will. All, including the State of Israel, stand accountable to God. The State of Israel is a geopolitical entity and is not to be validated theologically.

God's promise of land bears with it obligation. Land is to be used as the focus of mission, the place where a people can live and be a light to the nations. Further, because land is God's to be given, it can never be fully possessed. The living out of God's covenant in the land brings with it not only opportunity but also temptation. The history of the people of Israel reveals the continual tension between sovereignty and stewardship, blessing and curse.

The Hebrew prophets made clear to the people of their own day as well, indeed, as any day, that those in possession of "land" have a responsibility and obligation to the disadvantaged, the oppressed and the "strangers in their gates". God's justice, unlike ours, is consistently in favour of the powerless (Ps. 103:6). Therefore we, whether Christian or Jew, who affirm the divine promise of land, however land is to be understood, dare not fail to uphold the divine right of the dispossessed. We have indeed been agents of the dispossession of others. In particular, we confess our complicity in the loss of land by Palestinians, and we join with those of our Jewish sisters and brothers who stand in solidarity with Palestinians as they cry for justice as the dispossessed.

We disavow any teaching which says that peace can be secured without justice through the exercise of violence and retribution. God's justice upholds those who cry out against the strong. God's peace comes to those who do justice and mercy on the earth. Hence we look with dismay at the violence and injustice occurring in the Middle East.

For 3,000 years the covenant promise of land has been an essential element of the self-understanding of the Jewish people. Through centuries of dispersion and exile, Jews have continued to understand themselves as a people in relation to the God they have known through the promise of land. However, to understand that promise solely in terms of a specific geographical entity on the eastern shore of the Mediterranean is, in our view, inadequate.

"Land" is understood as more than place or property; "land" is a biblical metaphor for sustainable life, prosperity, peace and security. We affirm the rights to these essentials for the Jewish people. At the same time, as bearers of the good news of the gospel of Jesus Christ, we affirm those same rights in the name of justice to all peoples. We are aware that those rights are not realized by all persons in our day. Thus we affirm our solidarity with all people to whom those rights of "land" are currently denied.

We disavow those views held by some dispensationalists and some Christian Zionists that see the formation of the State of Israel as a signal of the end time, which will bring the Last Judgment, a conflagration which only Christians will survive. These views ignore the word of Jesus against seeking to set the time or place of the consummation of world history.

We therefore call on all people of faith to engage in the work of reconciliation and peace-making. We pray for and encourage those who would break the cycles of vengeance and violence, whether it be the violence of states or of resistance movements, of terror or of retaliation. We stand with those who work toward non-violent solutions, including those who choose non-violent resistance. We also urge nation states and other political institutions to seek negotiated settlements of conflicting claims.

The seeking of justice is a sign of our faith in the reign of God.

7. We affirm that Jews and Christians are partners in waiting. Christians see in Christ the redemption not yet fully visible in the world, and Jews await the messianic redemption. Christians and Jews together await the final manifestation of God's promise of the peaceable kingdom.

Explication

Christians' hope is continuous with Israel's hope, and is unintelligible apart from it. New Testament teaching concerning the Kingdom of God was shaped by the messianic and apocalyptic vision of Judaism. That prophetic vision was proclaimed by John the Baptist, and the preaching of Jesus contained the same vision. Both Jews and Christians affirm that God reigns over all human destiny and has not abandoned the world to chaos, and that, despite many appearances to the contrary, God is acting within history to establish righteousness and peace.

Jews still await the kingdom which the prophets foretold. Some look for a messianic age in which God's heavenly reign will be ushered in upon the earth. Christians proclaim the good news that in Christ "the Kingdom of God is at hand", yet we too wait in hope for the consummation of the redemption of all things in God. Though the waiting of Jews and Christians is significantly different on account of our differing perception of Jesus, nonetheless we both wait with eager longing for the fulfilment of God's gracious reign upon the earth — the kingdom of righteousness and peace foretold by the prophets. We are in this sense partners in waiting.

Both Christians and Jews are called to wait and to hope in God. While we wait, Jews and Christians are called to the service of God in the world. However that service may differ, the vocation of each shares at least these elements: a striving to realize the word of the prophets, and attempt to remain sensitive to the dimension of the holy, an effort to encourage the life of the mind, and a ceaseless activity in the cause of justice and peace. These are far more than the ordinary requirements of our common humanity; they are elements of our common election by the God of Abraham, Isaac and Jacob, and Sarah, Rebekah, Rachel and Leah. Precisely because our election is not to privilege but to service, Christians and Jews are obligated to act together in these things. By so acting, we faithfully live out our partnership in waiting. By so doing, we believe that God is glorified.

Recommendations

The Council of Theology and Culture makes the following recommendations to the 199th General Assembly (1987):

1a. That the General Assembly adopt for study and reflection the paper "A Theological Understanding of the Relationship Between Christians and Jews", and distribute it to the church as a provisional understanding of the subject along with a brief study guide including a bibliography and response questionnaire, the latter of which is to be returned to the appropriate ministry unit.

1b. That instruction be given to the appropriate ministry unit to appoint a work group composed of some members of the task force, some staff with responsibilities for work in the Middle East, and others to be chosen; and to invite Christians living in the Middle East to participate with the work group; that a conference be held with the Middle East Council of Churches and partner churches of the PC(USA) in the Middle East in the spring of 1988 to discuss and negotiate an acceptable understanding between the PC(USA) and the MECC and partner churches concerning its content, status and function in our ongoing work together; this committee is to report to the appropriate ministry unit at the conclusion of the conference.

1c. That instruction be given the appropriate ministry unit to report on the results of their study and reflection process and bring any appropriate recommendations to the 201st General Assembly (1989).

2. That the Stated Clerk be directed to print the report and to distribute it to each minister, Christian educator, and session within the church, to ecumenical partner churches in mission, to churches with which the Presbyterian Church (USA) is in correspondence, and to the major Jewish organizations in the United States; and partner churches of the PC(USA) in the Middle East.

3. That the General Assembly request pastors and Christian educators to initiate educational programmes designed to foster understanding and better relationships between Christians and Jews.
4. That the General Assembly urge the expansion of instruction in Judaic studies in the theological seminaries of the church.
5. That we communicate our sensitivity to the issue of including a Holocaust Remembrance Day in the liturgical calendar of the PC(USA) and to refer this matter to the appropriate ministry unit.
6. That the General Assembly instruct the General Assembly Council to give increased encouragement to those working for reconciliation of all parties in the Middle East through exploring the feasibility of joining with others, in as broadly an ecumenical way as possible, in developing those instrumentalities, acceptable to all participants, which enable and facilitate constructive dialogue and common efforts to improve relationships between Jews, Christians and Muslims, especially, but not only in the Middle East and the USA.
7. That the General Assembly Council be directed to monitor the implementation of these actions of the General Assembly and to report thereon periodically to the General Assembly.

The
Commentary

II

General Trends

A. Assemblies of the World Council of Churches

Close attention to positions relative to the Jewish people taken by Assemblies of the World Council of Churches since the founding of the WCC in 1948 reveals something of the last brief chapter in an almost 2000-year history of relationship between the Jewish and Christian communities. It is a far, far different chapter from most of those that preceded it.

1. The missionary movement

Though the documents here reproduced and thus the discussion of them begin with the First Assembly of the World Council of Churches in 1948, the chapter of which they are the most recent part began in the nineteenth century with the modern missionary movement. As missionaries accompanied and followed explorers, conquerors, and colonizers to almost every part of the then "unknown" world with the goal of bringing the gospel to everyone "in this generation" (to adopt a phrase made popular by John R. Mott at the turn of the twentieth century), they encountered people who apparently found complete satisfaction through their own, "non-Christian", religions. And the suspicion began to grow that perhaps God had ways with people that were different from those of Christianity. At the very least, the missionaries encountered people who were worthy of respect. Their religions, of course, were considered to be false but that could not be laid to their account: they simply had not had the opportunity to encounter Jesus Christ. The opportunity was now to be theirs.

Jews presented a special problem for missionaries, however, for Jews had never been without the opportunity to accept the gospel — unlike, for instance, Hindus, Buddhists, or traditional religionists. Further, Jews were neighbours of European and North American missionaries, not pagans "in some distant land". At the same time, the ancient scandal that the Jews continued to refuse to admit that Jesus was the Messiah remained and, with it, the urgency of their conversion. But, in contrast to earlier centuries, Jews as individuals, as human beings, were not considered degenerate or evil by the missionaries. On the contrary, felt love for Jews expressed itself in an intense desire to bring them the gospel and thus into the church. Because Christians loved the Jews, it was their Christian duty to convince them that the Messiah for whom they waited had already come. Indeed, one argument went, not to preach the gospel to the Jews was antisemitism itself.

That this nineteenth and early twentieth century attitude towards Jews represented a radical shift from that of preceding generations (when Jews, far from being loved, were actively hated and persecuted) cannot be emphasized enough. Perhaps the shift can be dated from the Enlightenment and then the Emancipation, when Jews were released from the ghettos and encouraged to become part of the general society. As Clermont-Tonnerre, a French philosopher, put it: "Everything should be denied to the Jews as a nation; everything should be granted to them as individuals." It therefore became tremendously important that individual Jews be converted to Christianity, while the concept of the Jewish *people* all but entirely vanished from consciousness.

The missionary movement was not the only "movement" concerning Jews current at the time, however. About the middle of the nineteenth century, politicians discerned that political capital could be gained by playing upon the animosity towards Jews inherited though the centuries when the church accused the Jewish people of deicide and ostracized it, and all within it, throughout Christendom. So the term "anti-Semitism" [1] came to mean hatred of Jews on what was supposed to be a racial basis, and politicians, imbuing it with honour, ran for office on anti-Semitic platforms. Jewish peoplehood, understood as "race", was paramount for the anti-Semitic movement; individual Jews were but instances of the Jewish "race", which was thought to be destined, through social Darwinism, to an eternally inferior place in society and history. Tragically, the "enlightened" missionary movement, with its emphasis on the individual Jew, was unable to muster the awareness necessary to counter racial and political anti-Semitism, with its negative emphasis on Jewish peoplehood ("race"), when the latter came to political power in the Third Reich.

For footnotes, see end of chapter, page 139.

For the missionary movement, however, antisemitism was anathema. Instead, love for "the Jews" was the order of the day. Under the auspices of the International Missionary Council and the leadership of John R. Mott, two conferences on "The Christian Approach to the Jews" were held in 1927, first in Budapest and then in Warsaw. The findings of the Budapest conference noted that: "Our message to the Jews is the love of God revealed in Jesus Christ, crucified, risen, glorified, the fulfilment of the Law and the true Messiah. He is the incarnate Word, the Redeemer of the world, the Saviour from sin, who is bringing Israel to her destiny — viz., to become a blessing to all humanity." [2]

Antisemitism was seen to be a dreadful evil. When the third conference on "The Christian Approach to the Jews" was held in Atlantic City, New Jersey (USA), in 1931, Dr Frank Gavin of the General Theological Seminary in New York could declare that "I do not believe that there is such a thing as 'religious antisemitism'... But when we look close into the cause of antisemitism, there is just enough color of the allegedly 'religious' element to make it seem plausible that it is a factor... For Judaism when practiced by observant Jews, certainly appears to the non-Jew a religion apart from the ordinary world. Within this quite limited meaning of the word 'religious intolerance' there is some basis for its existence, but the creating word, the determining factor, is not to be cast up to the gentile but to the Jewish side of the ledger." [3] In sum, antisemitism was blamed on the Jews themselves.

Nevertheless, the delegates to the 1931 conference, meeting as they were on the precipice of the Nazi terror, passed a short resolution that read: "We, the assembled delegates to the Atlantic City Conference on the Christian Approach to the Jews, associate ourselves in sympathy with the widespread suffering among Jewish peoples (sic) in Central and Eastern Europe and commend all well-directed efforts to provide relief to the support of Christian philanthropy." [4]

Whereas from the beginning of the Christian movement until the Enlightenment, the Jewish people had been a theological reality for the church, in the missionary movement it was de-theologized, becoming "the Jews" or "the Jewish peoples". As individuals, Jews were suitable targets for Christian evangelism while, at the same time, they were subjects of Christian compassion when they were oppressed, just as were other deprived or persecuted children of God. But, as the Jewish *people*, Jews were perceived to have no significance for Christian theology or ecclesiology.

Though Christian opposition to antisemitism could only be of benefit to the welfare of Jews, it provided a way for the church to sweep the theological significance of the Jewish people under the carpet. The otherwise laudable emphasis upon antisemitism as violation of human rights became, therefore, a substitute for wrestling with the critical issue of the theological significance of the Jewish people for Christian self-understanding. Misguided as it was, medieval persecution of Jews because they had "killed God" nevertheless took the Jewish people with theological seriousness, as the missionary movement, by and large, did not.

2. The Shoah

The Nazi attempt to eradicate the Jewish people led to some new thinking within the church that, while building upon the missionary perception of Jews, demonstrated the theological importance of Israel and, in particular, the theological significance of antisemitism. In a statement issued at Darmstadt on 8 April 1948, the Bruderrat of the Evangelical Church in Germany [5] declared:

> It may rightly be said that after what has happened, after all that we allowed to happen in silence, we have no authority to speak now. We are distressed about what happened in the past, and about the fact that we did not make any joint statement about it... Today when retribution is being meted out to us for what we did to the Jews, there is increasing danger that we may take refuge from God's judgment in a new wave of antisemitism, thus conjuring up all the old devils once again. In this perilous situation and amid this temptation God's word speaks to us and helps us to find the right attitude to the Jews.

But even though "the burning question of Judaism and the Christian church lies on our hearts like a stone", the German Protestants defined the "right attitude to the Jews" precisely as the missionary movement had done:

> The Bible tells us, and the Creeds of our Churches confirm, that Jesus of Nazareth was a Jew, a member of the chosen people, Israel... But the church is not allowed to teach that it makes no difference that Jesus is a member of the Jewish people, just as it is not allowed to ascribe him to any other nation or race...
>
> Since the Son of God was born a Jew, the election and destiny of Israel found its fulfilment in him...
>
> Since Israel crucified the Messiah, it rejected its own election and its own destiny...
>
> Through Christ, and since Christ, Israel's election has passed to the church, which is composed of all nations both Jews and Gentiles.

This understanding of the Jewish people led, however, to an insight about antisemitism that was absent in the missionary movement and, certainly, during the Nazi years. It is significant enough to warrant quoting in full:

> Because the church recognizes the Jew as an erring brother destined for Christ, a brother whom it loves and calls, it is not permissible for the church to regard the Jewish question as a racial or national problem, and to let that determine its attitude towards the Jewish people, or towards individual Jews. Furthermore, the church must show the world that the world is mistaken if it thinks it can settle the Jewish problem as if it were a racial or national one.
>
> It was a disastrous mistake when the churches of our time adopted the secular attitude of mere humanity, emancipation and anti-semitism towards the Jewish question. There was bound to be a bitter retribution for the fact that anti-semitism rose and flourished not only among the people (who still seemed to be a Christian nation), not only among the intelligentsia, and in governmental and military circles, but also among Christian leaders. And when finally this radical anti-semitism, based on racial hatred, destroyed our nation and our churches from within, and released all its brutal force from without, there existed no power to resist it — because the churches had forgotten what Israel really is, and no longer loved the Jews. Christian circles washed their hands of all responsibility, justifying themselves by saying that there was a curse on the Jewish people. Christians no longer believed that the promise concerning the Jews still held good, they no longer preached it, nor showed it in their attitude to the Jews. In this way we Christians helped to bring about all the injustice and suffering inflicted upon the Jews in our country.

The denial of "religious antisemitism" voiced by Dr Gavin in 1931 was rejected and responsibility of Christian teaching and doctrine for the Shoah acknowledged. But the theological understanding of the Jewish people remained that of the missionary movement. In the paragraph immediately following the one just cited, the German Protestants confessed "with shame and grief what a great wrong we have done to Israel, and how deep our guilt is. As a church we have failed to be the witness of salvation for Israel."

3. Amsterdam

This was the situation at the time of the World Council of Churches' founding Assembly in August/September 1948; the ambiguity in the churches about guilt for the Shoah and the desire to convert Jews was profound. The churches had come to a more accurate comprehension of antisemitism and their own involvement in it — and drew the conclusion that an even greater effort should be made to convert Jews to Christianity. A statement by the Protestant Commission on the Witness to Israel of the

Protestant Federation of France,[6] prepared for the WCC's First Assembly, summed it up:

> To the persecuted people, the church must say that their sufferings are not God's vengeance for the death of Jesus but an appeal to conversion and to turn from their unfaithfulness. It is obviously very hard to use this language to the survivors of the Nazi massacres. But Christians cannot attempt to proclaim the Gospel to the Jews unless they begin by affirming that Jesus really is the Christ, the Son of God, and that their unfaithfulness consists in their refusal to recognize him as the Messiah foretold in the prophets.

A shift was beginning to take place in Christian understandings of the Jewish people but only beginning. Years prior to Vatican II, the French Protestants appear to have been on the verge of rejecting the deicide charge, but they remained convinced that Jewish suffering — the Shoah! — is the consequence of Jewish refusal to recognize Jesus as the Messiah. It is not surprising, therefore, that the French paper should make the most explicit statement possible concerning the purpose of efforts at conversion:

> It follows that, unless we are to be at cross-purposes, a clear distinction should be drawn between anti-semitism and the anti-Judaism which is involved in every summons to conversion... The aim of general conversion cannot be anything less than the spiritual destruction of Judaism.

Thus, in the years immediately after the closing of the death camps very little changed in the church's theological perception of the Jewish people with the exception that awareness was growing of the Christian contribution to antisemitism. Christian mission to Jews, however, was seen to be more imperative than ever. At the same time, references to "the Jewish people" began to creep into church documents, often mixed with "the Jews" but nevertheless there. Change was coming — very slowly. The Shoah had placed "the Jewish question" squarely on the agenda of the church.

But the Shoah clearly was only part of the reason the churches were concerned about the "approach to the Jews". The other part was the missionary activity, and the theological issues thereby raised, carried out by the International Missionary Council and the organizations within it.

Both of these aspects are clearly evident in the statement "The Christian Approach to the Jews", that was debated and received by the Amsterdam Asssembly *(Doc. 1)*. Though the humanitarian concern for Jews as people who had suffered is present, the statement was discussed within a theological context. Thus its opening sentence constituted the beginning of a new *theological* approach to the Jewish people: "A concern for the Christian approach to the Jewish people confronts us inescapably, as we meet together to look with open and penitent eyes on man's disorder and to rediscover together God's eternal purpose for his church."

The statement then proceeds to note that: "No people in his one world have suffered more bitterly from the disorder of man than the Jewish people. We cannot forget that we meet in a land from which 110,000 Jews were taken to be murdered. Nor can we forget that we meet only five years (sic) after the extermination of 6 million Jews." The *very next* sentence then states unequivocally that "To the Jews our God has bound us in a special solidarity linking our destinies together in his design."

The church's "special relationship" with the Jewish people was made even more explicit in the second paragraph, where the delegates acknowledged: "In the design of God, Israel has a unique position. It was Israel with whom God made his covenant by the call of Abraham. It was Israel to whom God revealed his name and gave his Law..." [7] This insight from Amsterdam stands as the first and most basic of Assembly documents dealing with the Jewish people and may legitimately be the foundation upon which new efforts within the ecumenical movement can build forty years later.

The implications drawn from acknowledgment of Israel's special relationship with the church were those of the missionary movement:

> It was Israel to whom He promised the coming of his Messiah. By the history of Israel God prepared the manger in which in the fullness of time He put the Redeemer of all mankind, Jesus Christ. The church has received this spiritual heritage from Israel and is therefore in honour bound to render it back in the light of the Cross. We have, therefore, in humble conviction to proclaim to the Jews, "The Messiah for Whom you wait has come." The promise has been fulfilled by the coming of Jesus Christ.

This particular conclusion was not unanimously accepted by the delegates, however. [8] For instance, in plenary session Dr Herman Heering of the Remonstrant Brotherhood (Netherlands) moved that the entire statement be dropped: "It contained many telling statements, but to all who had at heart the sufferings of the Jews it must seem impossible to preach to a people which had gone through so much. They must first be given an opportunity of living at all." [9] But, by its vote to receive the statement, the majority agreed with Dr Benjamin Mays of the National Baptist Convention (USA) that it was imperative for the Jews to be brought "into full Christian fellowship here and now".

Thus the conclusion drawn from recognition of "the special meaning of the Jewish people for Christian faith" had only to do with that aspect of Christian faith contained in the Great Commission: "Go therefore and make disciples of all nations, baptizing them in the name of the Father and of the Son and of the Holy Spirit" (Matt. 28:19) — including, especially, Jews. And, since the relevant issue was understood to be how best to go about fulfilling that commission, some barriers had to be overcome, "particularly... the barriers which we have too often helped to build and which we alone can remove". The "barriers to be overcome" clearly were understood to be antisemitism. [10]

The paragraphs that follow were worded with a sensitivity and awareness of the actual nature of antisemitism that has seldom been repeated in ecumenical documents:

> We must acknowledge in all humility that too often we have failed to manifest Christian love towards our Jewish neighbours, or even a resolute will for common social justice. We have failed to fight with all our strength the age-old disorder of man which anti-semitism represents. The churches in the past have helped to foster an image of Jews as the sole enemies of Christ which has contributed to anti-semitism in the secular world.

Here we find that antisemitism is an "age-old disorder of man" and that the churches are at least partially responsible for "anti-semitism in the secular world." Further, the admission of failure to have a "resolute will for common social justice" gives evidence of future willingness to cooperate with Jews in the pursuit of justice and peace.

Then follow the sentences that were to be reiterated and *adopted* by the New Delhi Assembly in 1961 *(Doc. 3)*:

> We call upon all the churches we represent to denounce anti-semitism, no matter what its origin, as absolutely irreconcilable with the profession and practice of the Christian faith. Anti-semitism is sin against God and man. Only as we give convincing evidence to our Jewish neighbours that we seek for them the common rights and dignities which God wills for his children, can we come to such a meeting with them as would make it possible to share with them the best which God has given us in Christ.

In this section concerning antisemitism, which was entitled "Barriers to be overcome", the terms used for the subjects of antisemitism were "the Jews" and "our Jewish neighbours" — that is, Jews as individuals. But in the preceding section on "The special meaning of the Jewish people for Christian faith" and in the following one on "The Christian witness to the Jewish people" the reference is almost always collective. The earlier emphasis on the individual Jew was maintained with reference to anti-semitism, but virtually abandoned in terms of conversion. The call now was for conversion of the Jewish *people*. "In spite of the universality of our Lord's commission and of the fact that the first mission of the church was to the Jewish people, our churches have with rare exceptions failed to maintain that mission."

The fifth section has to do with "The emergence of Israel as a state". The Amsterdam Assembly delegates simply did not know how to respond to the Jewish people's claim to statehood. It adds, they said, "a political dimension to the Christian approach to the Jews and threatens to complicate anti-semitism with political fears and enmities". Certainly the state of Israel was to "complicate" the relation between the ecumenical movement and the Jewish people for a very long time to come. Nevertheless, in 1948 the Assembly elected to withhold judgment: "On the political aspects of the Palestine problem and the complex of 'rights' involved we do not undertake to express a judgment. Nevertheless, we appeal to the nations to deal with the problem not as one of expediency — political, strategic or economic — but as a moral and spiritual question that touches a nerve centre of the world's religious life."

This last sentence, extraordinary for its social and theological astuteness, became part of the statement as a consequence of deliberation in the Alternates' Committee IV; it was not in the original draft. The official report records the following:

> Dr Baines [Canon Henry Wolfe Baines, Church of England] thanked the chairman and the Assembly for allowing him, as an alternate, to speak in this matter. He was the more glad that this had been the case, as he wished to make a point agreed upon by the Alternates' Committee IV, dealing with the Jewish question. It was stated in the report that the Assembly had no wish to interfere with such questions at the government level, and with this the Alternates' Committee had been in entire agreement. But it was within the province of the Assembly, indeed it was the duty of the Assembly, to affirm to the responsible authorities of the nations concerned that this problem was more than a political one, it was spiritual. If the Assembly failed to say anything to that effect, the Alternates' Committee had held that it would be failing in its bounden duty, and missing *an opportunity never likely to recur* [emphasis added]. He wished to move an amendment to section V, to read as follows; beginning at the word "judgment": "... we appeal to the nations to deal with the problem not as one of expediency, political, strategic or economic, but as a moral and spiritual question that touches a nerve-centre of the world's religious life."

This amendment was accepted and integrated into the statement that ultimately was adopted. That Dr Baines and the Alternates' Committee felt the opportunity to deal with Israel as a "moral and spiritual" issue was a once-in-a-lifetime opportunity is indicative of their sensitivity to the political and historical situation. They made their appeal, and the Assembly accepted it.

4. The Christian approach to the Jews

After the International Missionary Council's conferences in Budapest, Warsaw and Atlantic City, a committee had been formed in 1931 related to the IMC called the Committee on the Christian Approach to the Jews. As a quasi-independent committee "sponsored" by the IMC, with its own constituency, independently-raised budget, and constitution, it was composed of representatives from organizations dedicated to Jewish mission, plus various other people with particular knowledge or expertise, including eventually (1951) representatives from the World Council of Churches.

Since the Committee on the Christian Approach to the Jews (IMCCAJ), which published a quarterly *Newsheet* and monitored the mainly European and North American missionary activity, was a "sponsored agency" of the International Missionary Council, its inclusion with the IMC in the proposed merger of that council with the World Council of Churches was not entirely automatic. As 1961 approached, when the merger was to occur, long and serious discussions were held within the IMCCAJ concerning the desirability of complete integration into the WCC. The arguments for integration included the observation that mission to the Jews was not a vital part of the WCC and that the committee could rectify that omission by being within the new Division of World Mission and Evangelism. The argument against was that some of the constituent organizations of the IMCCAJ would refuse to remain with the committee if it was in the World Council, and, moreover, the thrust of Jewish mission would be lost in the larger organization. In the end the decision was taken to integrate.

In taking that decision the IMCCAJ decided that the name of its successor committee should be the "Committee on the Church and the Jewish People". A search of IMCCAJ material in the WCC archives has so far failed to turn up records concerning the decision to recommend the name-change. But, prima facie, the change is highly significant, especially in light of the fact that the Committee on the Christian Approach to the Jews was almost exclusively oriented towards mission, which was the emphasis it wanted to maintain inside the World Council of Churches.

As has already been noted, the term (and the concept) "Jewish people" had slowly been finding its way into Christian discussion of Jews and Judaism. Consequently, a collection of essays published under the auspices of the IMCCAJ in 1954 was titled *The Church and the Jewish People*, edited by the committee's secretary, Göte Hedenquist. This volume, published just prior to the WCC's Second Assembly at Evanston, Illinois, USA, was designed both to implement the Amsterdam call (1948; *Doc. 1*) for more detailed study of the relations between Christians and Jews, and to prepare for the next Assembly.

It contained a remarkable selection of papers that, in their diversity, demonstrated the change in attitude that was beginning to be felt, at least in those parts of the church where the Jewish people was taken with theological seriousness. The missionary imperative was stated forthrightly, albeit with genuine concern for the Jews, by Bishop Stephen Neill, and the necessity for Jews as well as Christians to witness to their faith was emphasized by Rabbi Leo Baeck. Hans Kosmala, director of the Swedish Theological Institute in Jerusalem, discussed "State and Religion in the State of Israel". Few who are engaged in Jewish-Christian relations today would agree totally with many or most of the points made in these or others of the articles, though they represented breakthrough positions thirty years ago and must have produced discomfort in some churches. They were "clouds the size of a man's hand" that predicted the time when official church bodies would begin to take cognizance of the development of which they were a part.

5. Evanston and New Delhi

By 1954 the separation between those in the churches who were concerned for the theological significance of the Jewish people and those who saw Jews in solely political terms had already begun, a problem that became an issue at the Evanston Assembly of the World Council of Churches. Under the main theme, "Jesus Christ — the Hope of the World", came a sub-theme, "The Hope of Israel", which elicited one of the most divisive debates ever to take place at an Assembly. When time came for the discussion of the report on the main theme, efforts were made to delete all reference to Jews or to Israel on the basis that any such mention would be "a disservice to the cause of the World Council in the Near East", and rejection of "any suggestion that political events at present befalling the Jews were associated with the fulfilment of Christian hope". Despite some protests that there were no political implications in the idea that "Jesus Christ was born of Israel as fulfilment of the promises

God gave to His people", [11] the motion to eliminate all reference to Israel or Jews prevailed. The next day a minority report (1954; *Doc. 2*) was submitted by twenty-four theologians expressing the conviction that the Christian hope included hope for the conversion of Israel. This report was published as an appendix in the Assembly report.

Since the debate at Evanston was to prove critical for the understanding of the Jewish people within the ecumenical movement, Visser 't Hooft's comment on it is worth citing in full:

> What had happened? As the crucial vote was taken and I could clearly see from the platform what side the various national delegations were taking I said to myself: the spectre of Hitler is present. Not in the sense that anyone was infected by Hitler's anti-semitism. No, in a quite different way. I saw that the churchmen from countries which had been, for longer or shorter periods, under the national socialist regime had practically all come to feel that Israel had not only a central place in the past history of salvation, but also in the future of salvation. As they had had to face the demonic hatred of the Jews they had found deep meaning in St Paul's interpretation of the destiny of Israel in the ninth, tenth and eleventh chapters of the Epistle to the Romans. Those who had not been so close to the terrible drama of the extermination of Jews in Europe could not see it this way. They felt that to single out the Jews, to give them a special place in history, was — in spite of all good intentions — a sort of discrimination. It was their votes, together with the small number of votes from Near Eastern Christians who were afraid of political misunderstandings, which constituted the majority.
>
> There were some emotional reactions to the vote. But there was really no reason for anyone to feel self-righteous. The minority had to admit that before the days of Hitler they had practically all, including Karl Barth himself, interpreted St Paul's teaching on this point in a more or less allegorical rather than a historical way. And the majority had to learn that the minority had not the slightest intention of discriminating against the Jews, but was motivated by shame that the churches had not understood in time the full spiritual dimension of the Jewish question. This process of clarification would however take time. We would have to wait till the Third Assembly to arrive at a common statement on the subject.

Following the Evanston Assembly the WCC Central Committee asked that a consultation be held jointly with the IMC's Committee on the Christian Approach to the Jews on "Christian convictions and attitudes in relation to the Jewish people". This consultation was duly convened at the Ecumenical Institute at Bossey during September 1956, and its report, though presented to the Executive Committee, was not considered to be sufficiently representative of the churches and further study was requested. The report, however, was published in *The Ecumenical Review*, April 1956. In addition, some of the member churches of the World Council themselves conducted theological studies on the church and Israel (the results from the study conducted by the Ecumenical Council of the Hungarian Churches were particularly significant). These studies were filed in the World Council archives.

At New Delhi in 1961 (*Doc. 3*) the Assembly adopted a Resolution on Anti-Semitism, [12] which, in addition to emphasizing the Amsterdam denunciation and urging the member churches of the WCC "to do all in their power to resist every form of anti-semitism", took a gigantic theological step forward by rejecting the hoary charge of deicide against the Jewish people: "In Christian teaching the historic events which led to the Crucifixion should not be so presented as to fasten upon the Jewish people of today responsibilities which belong to our corporate humanity and not to one race or community." [13]

New Delhi was an important Assembly for the WCC: not only did the merger with the International Missionary Council take place but the Russian Orthodox and other Eastern Orthodox Churches became members. It was no occasion for acrimonious theological debate and the Council leadership made certain it did not happen. What did happen was described succinctly by Visser 't Hooft:

> This time the discussion on the Christian attitude to the Jewish people, on which the Evanston Assembly had not been able to find a common affirmation, led to a resolution which was adopted without opposition. We had learned our lesson. We knew that we could speak out together against anti-semitism, but that we had as yet no common mind about the theological questions of the destiny of the Jewish people or about the deeper significance of the creation of the state of Israel. So a resolution was proposed which was wholly concentrated on the issue of discrimination and which made the important point, that the historic events which led to the crucifixion should not be so presented as to fasten upon the Jewish people of today responsibilities which belong to our corporate humanity and not to one race or community. [14]

The debate on the resolution, however, revealed that several delegates were eager that the explicitly theological question, left hanging at Evanston, should be addressed in the antisemitism resolution. Rev. Christoph Schnyder of the Swiss Protestant Church Federation proposed an amendment that would have inserted the sentence: "On the contrary, the Jews remain God's chosen people (cf. Rom. 9-11), for even their rejection for a time must contribute to the world's salvation." At Visser 't

Hooft's urging, however, he withdrew the amendment and the debate was over. [15]

Since 1961 there has been no attempt to revive the question of the Jewish people's place within the ecumenical theological spectrum at a World Council of Churches Assembly.

6. Uppsala, Nairobi, and Vancouver

At the Fourth Assembly in Uppsala, Sweden, in 1968, barely one year after the Six-Day War, almost nothing was said about the "theological significance" of the Jewish people, despite the "Bristol document" of the Commission on Faith and Order (*Doc. 4*) from the year before, which reminded the churches that the creation of the State of Israel "is of tremendous importance for the great majority of Jews; it has meant for them a new feeling of self-assurance and security. But this same event has brought suffering and injustice to Arab people... We realize, however, especially in view of the changed situation in the Middle East as a result of the war of June 1967, that also the question of the present state of Israel, and of its theological significance, if any, has to be taken up."

Instead, the emphasis had shifted to the political situation in the Middle East and the concern was not for the Jewish people as such but about Israel's conflict with its Arab neighbours, under the general rubric as stated in the resolution, "Towards Justice and Peace in International Affairs": "The Word of God testifies that Christ takes the side of the poor and oppressed." [16]

The Statement on the Middle East (*Doc. 5*) asserted that the Assembly was "deeply concerned that the menace of the situation in the Middle East shows no present sign of abating. The resolutions of the United Nations have not been implemented, the territorial integrity of the nations involved is not respected, occupation continues. No settlement is in sight and a new armament race is being mounted." In addition, the statement insisted: "Full religious freedom and access to holy places must continue to be guaranteed to the communities of all three historic religions preferably by international agreement". [17]

Krister Stendahl, a delegate from the Lutheran Church in America who was later to become moderator of the Consultation on the Church and the Jewish People, introduced a motion to add an additional sentence to the statement: "It is the special responsibility of the World Council of Churches and of its member churches to discern ways in which theological and religious factors affect the conflict." A delegate from the Greek Orthodox Patriarchate of Antioch proposed that the word "theological" be removed, to which Stendahl demurred. Nevertheless, when put to a vote, the deletion was accepted, though the remainder of the sentence was incorporated into the statement. [18]

The mood and centre of attention at Uppsala relative to the Jewish people was radically different from what it had been at Amsterdam, Evanston, and even New Delhi. In 1967 the victory of Israel over the Arab armies had caught the attention of the world, including the churches. Twenty years before, the Amsterdam Assembly had not known what to say about the then new State of Israel, though it had appealed "to the nations to deal with the problem not as one of expediency — political, strategic, or economic — but as a moral and spiritual question that touches a nerve centre of the world's religious life". Stendahl's cautiously-worded addition to the Uppsala statement and its reception indicate that the Amsterdam plea *probably* would have got short shrift at Uppsala.

In 1975 at Nairobi, where the Assembly adopted two resolutions related to the State of Israel (one insisting on the sanctity of the holy places and another calling for cessation in the state of hostility between Israel and its neighbours), attempts to place Israel in an overtly theological context were defeated during debate — as were pleas by delegates from Middle Eastern churches for more explicit affirmation of the Palestinian cause. [19] So the Nairobi statement on the Middle East (*Doc. 6*) was devoid of any specifically theological or even religious reference. Instead it affirmed three points that would become the basis of future World Council policy: "Withdrawal by Israel from territories occupied in 1967; the right of all states including Israel and the Arab states to live in peace within secure and recognized boundaries; the implementation of the rights of the Palestinian people to self-determination." [20]

At Vancouver in 1983, the Sixth Assembly took positions about interfaith dialogue and mission, but nothing about the Jewish people as such. The statement on the Middle East, however, reflected an intensification of the theology that had informed the position taken at Uppsala and Nairobi: peace and justice through standing with the poor and oppressed. That statement (*Doc. 8*), the most recent Assembly statement dealing with the Jewish people, is worth careful consideration.

The introduction notes that the Middle East is the "birthplace of three monotheistic religions", and that the "churches in the area have their roots from apostolic times". These churches "are now facing new challenges and attempting to respond through new forms of witness". It therefore "behoves all churches to strengthen their presence and support their ministry, especially the ministry of reconciliation and witness for peace.

Historical factors and certain theological interpretations have often confused Christians outside in evaluating the religious and political developments in the Middle East." [21]

There can be little doubt that the phrase "certain theological interpretations" refers to a fundamentalist and millenarian Christian belief that the
return of the Jewish people to the land of Israel presages the second
coming of Christ, on the one hand, and, on the other, the theologies that
had developed within some WCC member churches concerning the
theological necessity of the Jewish people in their present reality (including the State of Israel) for Christian faith.

From then on the statement is an affirmation of the cause of the
Palestinians. The question of justice became entirely a question of justice
for the Palestinians — which was alleged to be delayed because of the
intransigence of Israel: "The Israeli settlement policy on the West Bank
has resulted in a *de facto* annexation, giving final touches to a discriminatory policy of development of peoples that flagrantly violates the
basic rights of the Palestinian people."

Assembly debate about the meaning of the Jewish people for the
theological self-understanding of the Christian church came to an end
with the ringing denunciation of antisemitism at New Delhi, which
poured oil on the troubled Evanston waters: no one since has wanted to
stir them again. But the theological importance of the Jewish people did
not vanish from the agenda of the World Council of Churches. Two
statements made by commissions of the WCC, both of which are
discussed in the pages that follow, could have made significant difference
had they figured in Assembly debate: the 1967 Bristol statement of the
Commission on Faith and Order (*Doc. 4*), and the statement prepared by
the Consultation on the Church and the Jewish People, which was
commended to the member churches by the WCC Executive Committee
in 1982 as "Ecumenical Considerations on Jewish-Christian dialogue"
(*Doc. 7*).

7. Conclusion

Throughout the common history of the church and the Jewish people
Jews have been *treated* as a people, while the *right* to be a people has
been denied. As we have seen, the church, until the mid-twentieth
century, officially taught that, while Jews had once been a people, they
were such no longer, for the Jewish people had been replaced by the new
people of God, the church. The Enlightenment welcomed Jews as
individuals while denying them peoplehood, following which the mis-

sionary movement loved Jews and, because they did, tried to convert them as individuals to Christianity. Antisemites, on the contrary, consider Jews to be a people, every member of which is equally abhorrent.

Some Christians and, through them, some ecclesiastical bodies, were shocked by the Shoah and the creation of the State of Israel into recognition that the genuine theological question was not the salvation of individual Jews nor prejudice against and persecution of Jewish individuals, but was, rather, the fact that the Jewish *people* existed and had the right to exist, both as a sociological and theological reality. The implications of that recognition (or the denial of it) for the faith of the church, profound as they are, are still being worked out in the theological positions of the ecumenical churches.

AB

NOTES

[1] The spelling "anti-Semitism" should be understood as a historical reference. In subsequent paragraphs the contemporary spelling, "antisemitism", will be employed, a spelling that does not imply discrimination against people who speak semitic languages, but precisely means hatred and persecution of the Jewish people.

[2] International Missionary Council, *The Christian Approach to the Jew*, London, Edinburgh House Press, 1927, pp.18f.

[3] International Committee on the Christian Approach to the Jews, *Christians and Jews*, New York & London, International Missionary Council, 1931, p.49.

[4] *Ibid.*, p.140.

[5] WCC archives.

[6] WCC archives.

[7] In following years ecumenical debate tended to deny the reality of any such special relationship: just six years later at Evanston, for instance, the argument was made that to understand the Jewish people in a special way was to discriminate against them!

[8] Though the statement on "The Christian Approach to the Jews" was "received" rather than "adopted" by the Assembly, it was thoroughly debated both in Committee IV and in full plenary session. At Amsterdam only matters having to do with such things as the WCC constitution were "adopted". Therefore, the category "received" carried more weight at the First Assembly than it was to bear in later WCC actions. The complete rubric was "received by the Assembly and commended to the churches for their serious consideration and appropriate action".

[9] For this and all subsequent references to plenary debate at Amsterdam see: W.A. Visser 't Hooft ed., *The First Assembly of the World Council of Churches*, London, SCM Press, 1949, pp.164ff.

[10] The official report of the 1948 Assembly used the spelling "anti-semitism", but the reprinting of the statement in the 1954 volume, *The Church and the Jewish People*, edited by Göte Hedenquist, secretary to the IMC's Committee on the Christian Approach to the Jews, adopted the spelling "antisemitism". Whether this change was happenstance or the result of conscious decision is not known.

[11] W.A. Visser 't Hooft ed., *The Evanston Report*, New York, Harper & Bros, 1955, p.78.

[12] W.A. Visser 't Hooft ed., *The New Delhi Report*, London, SCM Press, 1962, p.148.

[13] This sentence must certainly have been known four years later to the drafters of *Nostra Aetate*, the seminal statement by Vatican II on non-Christian religions. *Nostra Aetate*, paragraph 4, significantly improved on New Delhi by excluding Jews of Jesus' day from culpability for Christ's death: "Even though the Jewish authorities and those who followed their lead pressed for the death of Christ (cf. John 19:6), neither all Jews indiscriminately at that time, nor Jews today, can be charged with the crimes committed during his passion. It is true that the church is the new people of God, yet the Jews should not be spoken of as rejected or accursed as if this followed from holy scripture."

[14] *Memoirs*, Geneva, WCC Publications, 1987, 2nd ed., pp.313f.

[15] *The New Delhi Report, op. cit.*, p.149.

[16] Norman Goodall, ed., *The Uppsala Report 1968*, Geneva, WCC, 1968, p.61.

[17] *Ibid.*, p.189.

[18] *Ibid.*, p.188.

[19] By 1975 the tension between those who were concerned for the theological significance of the Jewish people — and thus of the Jewish state — and those who were concerned for justice for Palestinians had become acute. Neither was ready to acknowledge that the tension was unnecessary and mutually counter-productive.

[20] David M. Paton, ed., *Breaking Barriers: Nairobi 1975*, London, SPCK, 1976, pp.162f.

[21] David Gill, ed., *Gathered for Life: Official Report, Sixth Assembly, World Council of Churches*, Geneva, WCC, 1983, pp.147ff. All subsequent quotations from the Vancouver statement are from this source.

B. WCC Member Churches

As the World Council Assembly statements show (see A above), after the second world war a new epoch in Jewish-Christian relations, far different from all previous periods, began. New questions arose, new insights were achieved, and, step by step, a new theological agenda was developed. This movement is discernible even more clearly in the documents coming from different WCC member churches because, in contrast to the WCC itself, within the member churches the *theological* debate had developed more continuously.

1. As the dates of the documents indicate, there was a first period of intense theological reflection on the churches' relations to the Jews in the

years immediately after the war, which found its expression in a number of statements. Two main issues are treated in these documents:

A. *Antisemitism and Shoah (Holocaust)*. All the statements from those years took as their starting point what had happened to the Jews under the Nazis. This was seen as the result of antisemitism, which the Provisional Committee of the World Council in 1946[1] called "a denial of the spirit and teaching of our Lord", and which the First Assembly of the WCC at Amsterdam 1948 *(Doc. 1)* declared to be "sin against God and man", therefore "call(ing) upon all the churches... to denounce it".

In addition, the Amsterdam Assembly acknowledged that "the churches in the past have helped to foster an image of the Jews as the sole enemies of Christ, which has contributed to antisemitism in the secular world". It is not by chance that alongside the WCC it was the German church that in 1948 (see A above) and 1950 *(Doc. 9)* issued similar declarations on Christian responsibility for antisemitism, and thereby for the persecution of the Jews. Another statement of this kind had come in 1946 from the Hungarian churches[2] whose country and nation had been deeply involved in the events of the second world war, both on the side of the victims and of the collaborators.

B. *Mission to the Jews*. The other main concern to be found in the statements from this period is "to include the Jewish people in our evangelistic task". This was the first point explained by the Amsterdam Assembly in 1948 *(Doc. 1)* and the first of the "recommendations" given to the member churches of the WCC. The German church in 1948 appealed to its members: "Tell them (i.e. the Jews) that the promises of the Old Testament are fulfilled in Jesus Christ." And even "the fate of the Jews" was interpreted as "an admonition to the Jews to be converted to him, who is their sole hope of salvation". The Netherlands Reformed Church included this issue in its constitution of 1951 *(Doc. 10)*, making the distinction between "dialogue with Israel" and "mission... to the people in the non-Christian world". Yet the content of the dialogue shall be "to witness to them from the holy scripture that Jesus is the Christ".

2. It was more than fifteen years before the next public statement on Christian relations with the Jews and the Jewish people was made in the framework of the WCC and its member churches. Two times, at Evanston 1954 and at New Delhi 1961, the Assembly of the WCC failed to include this issue in its statements (see A above). The results of a consultation of the WCC on "Christian Convictions and Attitudes in Relation to the

Jewish People", held at Bossey in 1956 in conjunction with the International Missionary Council, were published in *The Ecumenical Review* (April 1956), but explicitly "not as a statement of the WCC".

Eventually, in 1967 at Bristol, a report of the Committee on the Church and the Jewish People was "accepted" by the Commission on Faith and Order and "commended for further theological study on a wider geographical scale" *(Doc. 4).* Apparently it became known only to limited circles within the WCC and its member churches, but there it had considerable impact because it raised a new set of issues.

A. *Common beginnings and parting of the ways.* The Bristol report was the first to look at the relations between Christians and Jews, and not only from a theological point of view: it took into consideration the historical developments that led to the separation of the two religious communities. It stated that "the first community of Christians were Jews who had accepted Jesus as the Christ", and that "they continued to belong to the Jewish communities". From this point of view it is evident that the beginnings of Christianity were characterized by closeness between the communities (see III.1 below), and that only later "the two groups of Jews broke apart as the consequence of various facts", some of those facts being of theological nature, while others were mainly social and political, as, e.g. the fact that "Christians of Gentile origin came greatly to outnumber the Jewish Christians".

Subsequent history shows an "ever increasing mutual estrangement", which was decidedly strengthened by the rise of Christianity as the accepted religion of the Roman state, and thereby participating in political power, while at the same time the Jews became a minority within the "Christian" state, often discriminated against and even persecuted (see III.B). This development led to a deep separateness between the two communities. The Bristol report said that "it is only since the beginning of this century, and even more especially since the last war, that churches... have begun to rethink more systematically the nature of their relationship to the Jews". Several statements and studies have taken up this approach, speaking of "common roots" and "parting of the ways" (see III.A and B).

B. *Continuity and discontinuity of Israel's election.* The traditional Christian position, which is reflected in virtually all documents from the first post-war period, holds the church to be the "new Israel" that had replaced the "old", i.e. the Jewish people. The Bristol report was the first to question the self-evidence of this position, describing a possible alternative: that both, Israel and the church, belong to the one people of God. In the meantime this position was accepted by many church bodies, in whose statements efforts were made to develop a new self-definition of the church that includes an acknowledgment of the continuity of Israel's election (see III.C.1 below).

C. *Mission or ecumenical dialogue?* The Bristol report also questioned the undisputed validity of the notion that, with regard to the mission of the church, there was no difference between Jews and gentiles. Instead, it explained the inter-relation of this question with ecclesiology:

> If the main emphasis is put on the concept of the church as the body of Christ, the Jewish people are seen as being outside. The Christian attitude to them is considered to be in principle the same as to men of other faiths and the mission of the church is to bring them, either individually or corporately, to the acceptance of Christ so that they become members of this body.
>
> If, on the other hand, the church is primarily seen as the people of God, it is possible to regard the church and the Jewish people together as forming the one people of God... (and to) say that the church should consider her attitude towards the Jews theologically and in principle as being different from the attitude she has to all other men who do not believe in Christ. It should be thought of more in terms of ecumenical engagement in order to heal the breach than of missionary witness in which she hopes for conversion (IV).

In principle, this position had been formulated already by the Netherlands Reformed Church (1951; *Doc. 10)*, which saw a difference between "dialogue with Israel" and "mission... to the people in the non-Christian world". The same position was expressed by the Evangelical Church of the Rhineland (1980; *Doc. 17)*:

> We believe that in their calling Jews and Christians are always witnesses of God in the presence of the world and before each other. Therefore, we are convinced that the church may not express its witness towards the Jewish people as it does its mission to the peoples of the world (4.6). [3]

3. The long-term impact of the Bristol report is clearly visible in later documents of the churches. Many of them chose a similar approach, beginning with the "common roots" *(Doc. 12 and 14)* or similar expressions of closeness and solidarity between Christians and Jews *(Doc. 11, 15 and 17)*, first of all stressing the commonalities, then asking for the reasons for the estrangement, and finally pleading for a renewal of mutual relations without any discrimination from either side.

Most documents emphasize that, notwithstanding the endeavours for a new relationship between Christians and Jews, a separateness continues to exist between the communities. They discuss what the reasons are for the continuing separateness, and to what degree they are inevitable or could and should be overcome.

A. *Jesus the Jew*. While it is obvious that the belief in Jesus as the Christ divides Christians and Jews from each other, only more recently the aspect of the Jewishness of Jesus, and the question whether this could be seen as a common or even a joining element, has been discussed by some churches. In this respect the discussion still is at its early beginnings.

While Jesus' Jewishness is expressed more and more without bias, or even with a positive connotation, the meaning of this fact for Jews and Christians respectively is still a point of debate. In particular the consequences for Christology as well as for other related theological topics, e.g. ecclesiology, are not yet elaborated. The Evangelical Church of the Rhineland (1980; *Doc. 17*) ventured a statement embracing several of the problems involved:

> We confess Jesus Christ the Jew, who as Israel's Messiah is the Saviour of the world and binds the peoples of the world to the people of God (4.3). We... realize that through Jesus Christ the church is taken into the covenant of God with his people (4.4).

Those statements can only be taken as first attempts to cope with this newly discovered problem of fundamental theological relevance. But they could serve as the opening of a new, important chapter of theological reflection that tries to draw some consequences from the new insights into the common roots of Jews and Christians for the crucial question of the meaning of Jesus in the context of Jewish-Christian dialogue. [4]

B. *The State of Israel*. One additional major new issue appeared on the agenda after 1967: the State of Israel. Though the state was already in existence at the time of the First Assembly of the World Council of Churches (1948), it only became an issue of debate following the Arab-Israel war of 1967.

A great difference is visible between the statements of the WCC itself (see A above) and those of some of the member churches with regard to Israel. While the WCC almost exclusively dealt with the political side of the matter, a number of churches tried to analyze the theological issues involved. One of the main questions is the relation of the Jewish people or nation to the land, biblical and post-biblical, and whether this should be looked at mainly from a historical and social or from a theological point of view. While several churches state a lack of consensus with regard to this question, the Evangelical Church of the Rhineland (1980; *Doc. 17*) expressed the insight that the continuing existence of the Jewish people, its return to the Land of Promise, and also the creation of the State of Israel, are signs of the faithfulness of God towards his people (2.3).

C. *Common responsibility*. Finally, several churches have begun to reflect on the question of what living together with mutual relations of Jews and Christians could mean for their common responsibility towards the world of today and its problems. Here the leading question is what we can learn from our common biblical tradition in order to face the issues of our time. One of the main points is the emphasis in the Hebrew Bible, as well as in the New Testament, that is laid on justice and peace. The realization of these goals is imperative for both Christians and Jews.

Another field of urgent actual problems is the relation of humanity to nature under the aspect of the threat to our world by exploitation and by unpredictable consequences of technological development. In this connection a misleading use of the biblical command to the first humans to "subdue" the earth and to "have dominion" over all creatures (Gen. 1:28) is often made. Therefore Jews and Christians are called to examine their common biblical tradition and to transfer their insights to public involvement in activities that are aimed towards solving the alarming problems of our day. [5]

RR

NOTES

[1] The World Council of Churches (in Process of Formation). Minutes and reports of the meetings of the Provisional Committee of the World Council of Churches held at Geneva, 21-23 February 1946, Geneva (no date), pp.33-36.

[2] Rolf Rendtorff and Hans Hermann Hendrix, eds, *Die Kirchen und das Judentum Dokumente 1945-1968*, Doc. E.II.2, Paderborn and Munich, 1988.

[3] For more detail on "Mission and Dialogue" see III.D.3.

[4] For more on these problems, see III.D.2.

[5] For more detail, see III.D.4.

III

Theological Issues

A. Common Roots

At Amsterdam 1948 (*Doc. 1*) the World Council of Churches declared:

> To the Jews our God has bound us in a special solidarity, linking our destinies together in his design.

This declaration was given in the face of the Shoah, which was mentioned immediately before. But at the same time it included a clear consciousness of the deep common roots of Jewish and Christian belief:

> In the design of God, Israel has a unique position.
> It was Israel with whom God made his covenant by the call of Abraham.
> It was Israel to whom God revealed his name and gave his law.
> It was to Israel that He sent his prophets with their message of judgment and grace.
> It was Israel to whom He promised the coming of his Messiah.

In 1977 the Norwegian Bishops' Conference (*Doc. 16*) declared:

> Historically and theologically, the church has a very near relation to the Jewish people. There the Christian faith has its roots.

The rediscovery of these common roots is fundamental to Christian self-understanding.

1. The common history of Jews and Christians begins with God's calling Abraham, Isaac and Jacob, the ancestors of Israel, revealing himself to them as the One God. This One living God, who is the Creator of heaven and earth, is known to us through his self-revelation to Israel. The God of Israel and the One God, whom we as Christians confess in the first article of our Apostolic Creed, is one and the same. The "Ecumenical Considerations on Jewish-Christian Dialogue" (1982; *Doc. 7*) spoke of

"the two communities, both worshipping the God of Abraham, Isaac, and Jacob" (2.10), and declared:

> The Christian church shares Israel's faith in the One God (2.11).

2. The revelation of this One God is given to us first of all through the Hebrew scriptures. They are *the* Bible of the Jews as they were *the* Bible of Jesus and his followers as well as that of the first generation of Christians. Regardless of certain differences in interpretation, even though at some points of major importance, they remain a common basis for faith and life of Jews and Christians. The Bristol report (1976; *Doc. 4*) said:

> The documents of the Old Testament belong to the heritage which the churches have received from and have in common with the Jews (v.1).

3. According to the Hebrew scriptures, one of the most important of God's communications with Israel was the giving of the Torah, which constitutes the centre of Jewish existence. The Bristol report said:

> (God) made himself known specifically to Israel, and showed this people what his will is for men on earth. Bound to him in love and obedience, it was called to live as God wants his people to live (III).

Jesus quoted from the Torah the commandments of love of God and love of the neighbour as the essence of God's will (Mark 12:33ff., par., cf. Rom. 13:9), and the Ten Commandments, which Jesus quoted as well (Mark 10:17ff., par.), constitute the indispensable basis for Christian life. A consultation of the Lutheran World Federation in 1982 [1] declared:

> Christians generally should learn that faith in Christ does not preclude but rather includes a fulfilment of the Torah in the love of Christ.

4. One of the significant elements which Christian faith inherited from the Hebrew scriptures is messianism. The prophets envisioned the coming of a messianic age, in which all suffering and injustice in the world will find its end (e.g. Isa. 11:1-9, 25:8). Jews and Christians are united in the hope for the ultimate coming of the Messiah, together with the coming of the messianic era. The Synod of the Evangelical Church of the Rhineland (*Doc. 17*) in 1980 said:

> We confess the common hope in a new heaven and a new earth and the power of this messianic hope for the witness and work of Christians and Jews for justice and peace in the world (4.8).

RR

---

[1] H. Croner, *Stepping Stones to Jewish Christian Relations*, London/New York, 1977, pp.85f.

B. *The Parting of the Ways*

The rediscovery of the common roots leads to the awareness that at the beginning Christians and Jews had a common history. The Bristol report (*Doc. 4*) in 1967 was the first document in the framework of the WCC to emphasize the importance and necessity of historical considerations as a basis for theological insights. It said:

> The first community of Christians were Jews who had accepted Jesus as the Christ. They continued to belong to the Jewish communities and the relationship between them and their fellow-Jews was close, notwithstanding the tension that existed between them (II).

1. It is an obvious and undeniable historical fact that the first Christians were Jews and that they remained members of the Jewish people and understood their own faith as being fully within that tradition. That means that in the beginning of Christian history there were no "Christians" as distinct from "Jews", but within the Jewish community there existed one group, alongside others (as, e.g. Pharisees, Sadducees, Essenes, etc.), whose members believed that in Jesus the Messiah already had come.

2. But in the course of time a tension between them arose,

> a tension caused by the fact that the Christian Jews believed that the fullness of time had come in Christ and in the outpouring of the Spirit and that they therefore came to know themselves to be found in one fellowship with Gentiles who also believed in God through Jesus Christ (*Doc. 4*).

This inclusion of gentiles constituted a fundamental change in the character of the Christian community. It could no longer remain an integral part of the Jewish people but had to develop its own identity. As "Christians of Gentile origin came greatly to outnumber the Jewish Christians" (*Doc. 4*), the Christian community came increasingly and necessarily to see itself as being distinct from the Jewish people. Further, it also saw itself as having displaced the Jewish people in God's favour, a development that was to have destructive consequences.

3. Several factors worked together to accelerate the separation of Christians and Jews and to widen the gap between them. First of all the political developments deeply changed the situation in the land of Israel (which the Romans then began to call "Palestine", "land of the Philistines"). The Roman-Jewish wars (66-74 and 132-135 C.E.) with their disastrous results, mainly the destruction of Jerusalem and the temple

(70 C.E.), had several consequences, among them the dispersion of the Jewish-Christian community of Jerusalem and the consolidation of Rabbinic Judaism as the one surviving Jewish faction — which became formative and even normative for the subsequent Jewish tradition. From then on one "Christianity", i.e. the mainly gentile Christian community, and "Judaism", i.e. the Rabbinic Judaism as constituted at Javne (Jamnia), existed as two clearly defined and distinct entities — a constellation that had been non-existent in the time of the first generation of the Christian community.

4. The mutual estrangement, then, had its historical roots in the increasing gentile character of the church and the deepening concern of the Jewish leaders to unify and rebuild their people around fidelity to Torah. These developments resulted in a different self-understanding of the two communities (see III.A.1 and III.C.1), as well as in different views of Israel's scriptures (see III.A.2 and III.C.2), and of course in different views of Jesus and messianism (see III.A.4 and III.C.4).

5. While in the first centuries both Judaism and Christianity had been minority religions within the Roman Empire, the situation changed dramatically at the beginning of the fourth century when the emperor Constantine turned to Christianity. The Bristol report (*Doc. 4*) noted that:

> After Christianity became the accepted religion of the Roman state, the Jews were discriminated against and often even persecuted by the "Christian" state, more often than not with ecclesiastical support.

This coalition of Christian religion and political power led, through many terrible anti-Jewish excesses during the Middle Ages, to modern anti-semitism with its gruesome consequences (see III.D.1).

6. As explained earlier (II.A), the Nazi attempt to eradicate the Jewish people (the Shoah) caused some new thinking within the churches. In February 1946, the Provisional Committee of the World Council of Churches (in Process of Formation) [1] recorded its

> deep sense of horror at the unprecedented tragedy which has befallen the Jewish people in consequence of the Nazi attempt to exterminate European Jewry.

---

[1] The World Council of Churches (in Process of Formation). Minutes and reports of the meeting of the Provisional Committee held at Geneva, 21-23 February 1946, Geneva (no date), pp.33-36.

It urgently called upon Christians throughout the world

> to combat this evil by all the means within their power and especially... by testifying against the principles and practices of Antisemitism as a denial of the spirit and teaching of our Lord.

In addition the First Assembly of the WCC, held in Amsterdam in 1948 (*Doc. 1*), acknowledged:

> The churches in the past have helped to foster an image of the Jews as the sole enemies of Christ, which has contributed to anti-semitism in the secular world. [2]

Some churches went even further, confessing a Christian guilt or co-guilt for the Shoah. This confession is not only to be found in statements by German church bodies, such as the Synod of the Evangelical Church in Germany (*Doc. 9*) and the synod of the Evangelical Church of the Rhineland in 1980 (*Doc. 17*), but also in some declarations by non-German churches as, e.g., the United Methodist Church (USA) (*Doc. 12*), which declared in 1972:

> Christians... are obliged to examine their own implicit and explicit responsibility for the discrimination against and for organized extermination of Jews, as in the recent past.

Recently also the "Ecumenical Considerations on Jewish-Christian Dialogue" (1982; *Doc. 7*) acknowledged:

> Teachings of contempt for Jews and Judaism in certain Christian traditions proved a spawning ground for the evil of the Nazi Holocaust.

There is now general agreement that Christians not only have to avoid antisemitism but that they have to fight it wherever they meet it, be it inside or outside the churches.

In addition, from several documents it becomes evident that the awareness of Christian involvement in antisemitism with its terrible consequences can serve as an eye-opener to discern certain wrong developments in Christian thinking about Jews and Judaism. A consultation of the Lutheran World Federation [3] in 1964 spoke about "the long terrible history of Christian culpability for anti-semitism" and declared:

---

[2] The Third Assembly, held at New Delhi in 1961 (*Doc. 3*), "recalled" the First Assembly's demand "to denounce anti-semitism" without mentioning the above-quoted acknowledgment of Christian contribution to it (see II.A).

[3] See III.A.3, note 1.

"No Christian can exempt himself from involvement in this guilt." As a result the consultation "urge(d) the Lutheran World Federation and its member churches":

> To examine their publications for possible anti-semitic references, and to remove and oppose false generalizations about Jews. Especially reprehensible are the notions that Jews, rather than all mankind, are responsible for the death of Jesus the Christ, and that God has for this reason rejected his covenant people.

This consciousness, that it is now an urgent task to re-examine Christian theological traditions in the light of Christian involvement in and responsibility for antisemitism, and by that finally for the Shoah, is an important element in the current debate on a renewal of the Christian attitude towards Jews and Judaism.

RR

C. Traditional Theological Issues

The newly awakened thinking (see III.B.6 above) poses a challenge to much traditional theological thought. It becomes evident that in some cases the same issues, which have been recovered as the common roots of Jewish and Christian faith, include traditional Christian prejudices, which constitute the main obstacles to a renewal of the Christian attitude to Jews and Judaism. The Bristol report (1967; *Doc. 4*) described this as follows:

> Christians generally thought... in very stereotyped ways: the Jews as the Israel of the Old Testament had formerly been God's elect people, but this election had been transferred to the church after Christ; the continuing existence of the Jews was primarily thought of in terms of divine rejection and retribution, because they were regarded as those who had killed Christ and whose hearts were so hardened that they continued to reject him (II).

Here first of all the problem of covenant and election is at stake: Is Israel (or the Jewish people) still God's elect people as it originally was according to the testimony of the Hebrew scriptures? Or is "the church replacing Israel as God's people", as the "Ecumenical Considerations" (1982; *Doc. 7*, 2.3) describe a "classical Christian tradition"? What then about God's covenant with God's people?

The question of understanding scripture enters in. Since the Hebrew scriptures have been recovered as a common basis for faith and life for Jews and Christians (see III.A.2), the question arises whether the Christian interpretation of the "Old Testament" is the only legitimate one. How shall Christians evaluate the fact that there is a continuous Jewish tradition of interpretation of the Hebrew scriptures that is not at all aimed towards their fulfilment in Jesus Christ? What is the meaning of "Old" and "New"?

Related is the question of the Torah. Is Judaism "a fossilized religion of legalism", as the "Ecumenical Considerations" describe a common Christian prejudice? How can Christians achieve an appropriate view of the Jewish understanding of Torah? Is "law" an adequate expression? How do we have to understand Jesus' relation to the Torah? And that of Paul? What is the meaning of the Torah for Christians today?

Finally, the understanding of Jesus is one of the central issues. What is the significance of the fact that Jesus was a Jew — as were all his disciples and followers? Especially, does Jesus' Jewishness have implications for the church's Christology? Could or should the church learn about Jewishness, and so about Jesus as a Jew, from Jews today? And is the Jewish concept of the Messiah appropriate for what the church wishes to claim about Jesus?

One common denominator of all these issues is the question as to whether and how those elements coming from our common roots necessarily must divide Christians and Jews from one another — or whether they can relate us to each other or even unite us.

1. Covenant and election

a) Until recently it had been a common Christian conviction that Israel's election as the people of God and the covenant that God made with Israel had come to an end; the church had replaced Israel. It is obvious that this judgment of Israel (or the Jewish people) is a reflection of Christian self-definition as the sole elected people of God. The Jewish people had to give way to the Christian church. The "Ecumenical Considerations" (1982; *Doc. 7*) described the situation as follows:

> As Christianity came to define its own identity over against Judaism, the church developed its own understandings, definitions, and terms for what it had inherited from Jewish traditions, and for what it read in the scriptures common to Jews and Christians. In the process of defining its own identity the

church defined Judaism, and assigned to the Jews definite roles in the understanding of God's acts of salvation. It should not be surprising that Jews resent those Christian theologies in which they as a people are assigned to play a negative role (1.5).

b) The conviction that the church had replaced Israel as the elected people found its explicit expression in some documents, as e.g. the statement by the German Bruderrat[1] which in 1948 declared:

> The election of Israel through and since Christ has passed to the church, which is composed of all nations, both Jews and Christians.

Yet in contrast to that another German document, by the Synod of the Evangelical Church in Germany (*Doc. 9*), declared in 1950:

> We believe that God's promise to the people of Israel which He elected is still in force, even after the crucifixion of Jesus Christ.

This latter view is clearly expressed as one of two positions in the Bristol report (1967; *Doc. 4*):

> Others of us are of the opinion that ... after Christ the one people of God is broken asunder, one part being the church, which accepts Christ, the other part Israel outside the church, which rejects him, but which even in this rejection remains in a special sense beloved by God. They see this election manifested specifically in the fact that the existence of the Jewish people in this world still reveals the truth that God's promises are irrevocable, that he will uphold the covenant of love which he has made with Israel (III).

With reference to the words of Paul: "I ask, then, has God rejected his people? By no means!" (Rom. 11:1), the General Synod of the Netherlands Reformed Church (*Doc. 11*) in 1970 declared:

> Because God's election is based solely on his own faithfulness, this people remains even now the chosen people, and their sonship and the promises given are still valid.

c) Many recent documents stress that the election of Israel, which is expressed in many ways in the Hebrew Bible, is still valid. Thereby the theological question arises as to how to determine the self-definition of the church in its relation to Israel. This question includes the problem of an appropriate use of the concepts of covenant and people of God.

---

[1] See II.A.

The Texas Conference of Churches (1982; *Doc. 18*) stressed the importance of the notion of covenant but left the question open how precisely to define its nature:

> Jews and Christians share a common calling as God's covenanted people. While we differ as to the precise nature of the covenant, we share a common history and experience of God's redemptive presence in history. Both Jews and Christians are called to the covenant as they understand it.

Another approach to the problem is to say that "the people of God is broken asunder" (Bristol 1967; *Doc. 4*, III). In this conception the church is seen as belonging to and even being a part of the people of God. A similar view is to be found in the statement of the General Assembly of the Presbyterian Church (USA) (1987; *Doc. 20*):

> We affirm that the church, elected in Jesus Christ, has been engrafted into the people of God established by the covenant with Abraham, Isaac, and Jacob. Therefore, Christians have not replaced Jews.

Here the two terms, covenant and people of God, are used together, meaning virtually the same. The Synod of the Evangelical Church of the Rhineland (1980; *Doc. 17*) tried to make a distinction between them, saying.

> We believe in the permanent election of the Jewish people as the people of God and realize that through Jesus Christ the church is taken into the covenant of God with his people (4.4).

This differentiation tries to avoid saying either that the church owns the title "people of God", taking it away from Israel, or that Christians claim to be members of the people of Israel, which is defined by its national history. The distinction between "people of God" and "covenant" tries to do justice to both sides: Israel remains *the* people of God, as it is expressed frequently in the Hebrew Bible and in the New Testament as well (e.g. Luke 2:32, Rom. 9:4, 11:1); yet the covenant has been enlarged to include those gentiles who, through Jesus Christ, share in the promises of the Hebrew Bible. This includes the eschatological hope that one day both Jews and gentiles will definitely be united as the one people of God.

d) Further theological reflection is needed in order to find appropriate definitions and language to express the relations between Israel and the church. Yet the first fundamental step has been taken by many church bodies to express definitely that they will not continue to declare that

Israel's election has been transferred to the Christian church. This includes the relinquishment of any thoughts or expressions of Christian superiority to Jews and the Jewish people.

God first established the particular covenant with Abraham as the father of the Jewish people; but at the same moment God declared: "By you all the families of the earth shall be blessed (or: bless each other)" (Gen. 12:3). The church sees this promise confirmed in the calling of the gentiles into this covenant, to which they have immediate access through Jesus Christ.

RR

2. The scriptures

The Hebrew scripture is the Bible of the Jews as it was the Bible of Jesus, his first followers, and the early Christian church. The Hebrew scripture belongs to the common roots of both Jews and Christians (cf. III.A). Jews speak of Tenach, Christians of Old Testament.

a) The 1967 Bristol report voices an important warning:

> There is general tendency among Christians to equate the faith of the Old Testament with Jewish religion today. This is an oversimplification which does not do justice to Jewish understanding of the Old Testament and to subsequent developments.

The written Torah, consisting of the five books of Moses, but for Jewish understanding also the whole Tenach, is the substance of the covenant between God and Israel. The oral Torah, written down in the Talmud, is, according to the Rabbis, as much God's revelation from Sinai as is the written Torah. The "Ecumenical Considerations" (*Doc. 7*) from 1982 state:

> Judaism, with its rich history of spiritual life, produced the Talmud as the normative guide for Jewish life, in thankful response to the grace of God's covenant with the people of Israel. Over the centuries important commentaries, profound philosophical works and poetry of spiritual depth have been added. For Judaism the Talmud is central and authoritative. Judaism is more than the religion of the scriptures of Israel.

b) The Christian scripture consists of the Hebrew Bible (the "Old Testament" — the Greek translation, the Septuagint canon, comprises a larger body of Jewish wisdom and apocalyptic literature than the Hebrew canon) and the writings of the apostolic community (the "New Testa-ment"). The apostles and the early church interpreted parts of the Hebrew scripture in a new way. Jesus — his life, teaching, death, and resurrection — was the heart of their faith. Ultimately this faith led to a radical reinterpretation of the Hebrew scripture. So, the church understood the Jewish Bible, its "Old Testament", as a preparation for and a prefiguring or type of that which came in its fuller clarity only in the "New Testament". The scripture of Israel was therefore never accorded the standing which it had and has for Jews and had for Jesus.

As long ago as the second century Marcion had proposed that the church dispense with the Old Testament. He regarded the God of the Old Testament as a strange and cruel God and he saw in Jesus the absolutely new beginning of the revelation of God's love. His views were officially rejected by the church. A latent Marcionism, however, remained in the church through all the centuries of Christian history, though officially the Old Testament became and continued to be part of its canon.

c) Jewish faith and *halacha* (norms for the way of life) are based on Tenach as interpreted in the ongoing tradition of the Jewish people. The church follows another tradition in the interpretation and actualization of the Hebrew Bible. In the "Ecumenical Considerations" (*Doc. 7*) this is described as follows:

> For Christians the Bible with the two Testaments is also followed by traditions of interpretations, from the church fathers to the present time. Both Jews and Christians live in the continuity of their scripture and Tradition.

In Jewish-Christian dialogue as well as in ecumenical theological encounter the question of the relation between scripture and Tradition is in the forefront. The Bristol report (*Doc. 4*) strikes here an important note:

> When this problem, which has been a cause of dissension between Chris-tians for a long time, is considered in this new setting (i.e. in Jewish-Christian dialogue), the churches may gain insights which can contribute to a greater understanding and agreement among themselves.

d) Although the Hebrew scriptures ("Old Testament") are fully recog-nized in the church as part of the canon, the New Testament is regarded as the *fulfilment* of the Old Testament in the words of the Bristol report:

> We believe that in Jesus Christ God's revelation in the Old Testament finds its fulfilment. Through him we see into the very heart of God, in him we see

what it really means to say that God is the God of the covenant and loves man to the very end.

As soon as Christian theology uses "fulfilment" terminology, the danger is always present that the Old Testament will be regarded as superseded by the New Testament and the Jewish people as replaced by the Christian church. It seems appropriate to add to the "fulfilment" terminology the concept of "confirmation". In a study paper of the Commission on Faith and Order of the WCC ("The Significance of the Old Testament in its Relation to the New", Geneva, 1978) this theme is elaborated:

> Christ's fulfilment of the Old Testament promises should not just be interpreted in terms of realization but also in terms of confirmation. The promises and expectations of the Old Testament are often fulfilled in such totally unexpected ways, that in their fulfilment they appear to have received a radical reinterpretation; often they can only be recognized as being fulfilled in Christ on the basis of this reinterpretation.

The Synod of the Evangelical Church of the Rhineland (*Doc. 17*) tried to avoid the use of the word "new", which could be directed against the Jewish people:

> We want to perceive the unbreakable connection of the New Testament with the Old Testament in a new way, and learn to understand the relationship of the "old" and the "new" from the standpoint of the promise: as a result of the promise, as confirmation of the promise. "New" means therefore no replacement of the "old". Hence we deny that the people Israel has been rejected by God or that it has been superseded by the church.

In a 1967 declaration of the Belgian Protestant Council on Relations between Judaism and Christianity [2] we find that:

> Neither in the scriptures nor in the apostolic writings is there a break between "old" and "new".

In a footnote the Belgian Protestant Council added:

> It is not correct to designate the Torah, the Prophets and Writings (in abbreviated form the three together are called Scriptures) as "Old Testament", and the Apostolic Writings as "New Testament". This terminology suggests an opposition or contrast that does not exist.

---

[2] H. Croner, *More Stepping Stones to Jewish-Christian Relations*, 1985, pp.193-197.

e) In the study paper on "The Significance of the Old Testament in its Relation to the New" (1978) the specificity of the Old Testament is formulated as follows:

> It is mainly from the Old Testament that we come to know God as the Creator of all, that is, as the Lord of history, as the Judge who upholds the rights of the poor and the downtrodden. There too his holiness, majesty and hiddenness are emphasized, his concern with world politics, his exclusive claim upon his creatures and what the Old Testament calls his jealousy. Other specifically Old Testament notions are the creation of man and woman in the image of God, their place in the cosmos as God's caretakers, and the much greater attention given to nature; the warning against the constant temptation to idolatry, the fight against the deification of any part of creation and the danger of a dead, formal religion; moreover the interest in social structures, the insistence on righteousness, the fight against poverty and oppression, the concern with sorrow and the complaint of having been forsaken by God, and the importance of faith in providing wisdom for everyday life.

The Old Testament means more for Christians than just as a testimony to the preparation for the coming of Christ. It is certainly important that the Old Testament provides a context for the New Testament, but its significance goes beyond that fact. The Old Testament has a validity of its own.

f) Sometimes Christians have maintained that the Old Testament is only a kind of foreword to the gospel and could be replaced by the prehistory of other peoples. If so, the historicity of actual Israel, past and present, would be ignored. Israel would become only a symbol or an example of how God is at work among the nations in a redemptive way. The Bristol report (*Doc. 4*) would appear to warn against such an interpretation:

> The Old Testament is not only of importance for those whose culture is to a greater or lesser degree rooted in it, but becomes also the spiritual heritage of those Christians whose own ethnic culture is not touched by it.

In the report of the consultation of the Lutheran World Federation (1982) this theme is also mentioned:

> The sacred writings of other peoples do not replace the Old Testament. Yet religious traditions from outside the Judeo-Christian heritage may at times provide resources to enhance the articulation of the gospel in new contexts, as they have in past periods of church history.

And further:

> In the encounter with Judaism and the Jewish people the church gains a
> fuller sense of its own biblical roots, which may be the starting point of the
> process of contextualization.

g) An important question is still open for theological reflection: what is
the theological significance for Christians of the historical conclusion that
two religious traditions came from the Hebrew scriptures? Is the Christian
interpretation of the Hebrew scriptures sufficient or have Christians
something to learn from an independent Jewish interpretation of the
Hebrew scriptures after Christ?

In a recent publication, *Jewish Questions!... Christian Answers? An
Attempt at Dialogue* (1987) by the Committee on Church and Israel of the
Reformed Churches in the Netherlands, received by the Synod, this
theme is touched:

> That Jews and Christians interpret the scriptures of Israel from different
> perspectives, will remain the subject of intensive dialogue till the end of time,
> just as it was during the time of the apostles. Probably both Jews and Christians
> will in the future rejoice in the revelation of the inscrutable ways of God. In the
> meantime each will have to recognize that the other is engaged in the interpreta-
> tion of the same scriptures, which are the basis for both communities. Elements
> of truth therein should be recognized reciprocally. After a long history the
> church should be the first to take that step. The church should recognize that for
> Jews Torah and Tradition are a full message of grace and truth.
>
> SSch

3. Torah and law

a) The term "Jewish legalism" reflects one of the most fundamental
Christian prejudices against Jews. Many times it has been used as *the*
characterization of Judaism as opposed to Christianity. "Law" is taken as
the specific Jewish element, while Christianity is characterized by
"grace". Popular Christian theology, which claims to be based on Paul's
teaching, has claimed that Jewish endeavours to fulfill the law are but an
attempt to achieve salvation by one's own efforts, while Jesus freed men
and women from this impasse by offering salvation by pure grace.

Yet as long ago as 1948, the WCC's Amsterdam statement (*Doc. 1*)
spoke in different terms:

> It was Israel to whom God revealed his name and gave his law.

Here the law is seen in a positive way as a divine gift along with the
revelation of his name. A consultation of the Lutheran World Federation

(1982)[3] tried to explain the Jewish understanding of the Torah to Christians:

> For Jews the Torah... is a record of a covenant between God and his people that is still in force. Every Jew is under obligation to participate actively in this covenant by living according to the will of God as expressed in the Torah.
>
> Christians should realize that this Jewish understanding is not necessarily legalistic but may lead to a life in the presence of God. Those early Christians generally should learn that faith in Christ does not preclude but rather includes a fulfilment of the Torah in the love of Christ.

b) In the last statement we find some basic questions raised and answered:

— The Torah is an integral part of God's covenant with Israel. The covenant is God's gracious gift, and as a response to it all Israel and individual Jews are called to fulfill the divine commandments. Therefore the word "law" is not an appropriate rendering of the Hebrew word *torah*, especially not in the religious sense that has been given to it by Christian tradition. Torah means "teaching" or "instruction": how to live within the covenant that God has established. The notion that one could earn salvation by fulfilling the Torah is not a Jewish idea.

— Jesus himself lived according to the Torah and never questioned it. On the contrary: "Think not that I have come to abolish the law and the prophets; I have come not to abolish them but to fulfill them" (Matt. 5:17). Several times he discussed questions of the law with "Scribes and Pharisees", and the Gospels show that Jesus' interpretation of the Torah was within the contemporary Jewish discussion (e.g. Matt. 12:1-8,9-14).

— The early Jewish Christians remained members of the people, obedient to the Torah. Only when gentiles entered the Christian community did the problem arise as to whether or not they also should be obliged to fulfill all the commandments of the Torah. This problem was discussed by Paul and the representatives of the Jewish Christian community in Jerusalem (Gal. 2:1-9, cf. Acts 15) and finally solved by an agreement that gentile Christians should be obliged only to observe those commandments that are given to all humankind (cf. e.g. Gen. 9:4).

---

[3] See III.A.1.c., note 1.

c) Christians should realize that for Jews the Torah consists of two parts: the Hebrew Bible or *Tenach*, in particular the five books of the Pentateuch (Genesis to Deuteronomy), called the "written Torah", and the continued interpretations of the written Torah in the Talmud, which are called the "oral Torah". The "Ecumenical Considerations" (1962; *Doc. 7*) explains as follows:

> Judaism, with its rich history of spiritual life, produced the Talmud as the normative guide for Jewish life in thankful response to the grace of God's covenant with the people of Israel (2.8).

Covenant and Torah form an indissoluble unity. This includes the continuous interpretation of the biblical laws through the centuries, according to the needs of a changing life. Thus Judaism is not a petrified legalistic system, but to live according to the Torah for a Jew means a permanent vivid endeavour to fulfill the commandments within daily life and work.

d) For Christians the Torah cannot be compulsory as it is for Jews. In particular, those parts of the Torah that are related to certain cultic and ritual aspects of the Jewish religion only can have their relevance within the framework of this religion itself. This includes a certain Jewish way of life that is characterized by the observance of the rules for kosher food, purity, Sabbath and holidays, etc.

But in the field of ethics the Torah is of basic relevance for Christians as well as for Jews. Jesus, interpreting particular aspects of behaviour towards the neighbour (Matt. 5:20ff.), called the commandment, "You shall love your neighbour as yourself" (Lev. 19:18) one of the greatest of the commandments, together with the other one, "You shall love the Lord your God with all your heart..." (Deut. 6:5), adding: "On these two commandments depend all the law and the prophets" (Matt. 22:34ff.). Paul used a similar concentration of the whole law (Rom. 13:8-10, Gal. 5:14). This shows that for both of them the Torah was the basic source for any rule of Christian life.

In the history and tradition of Christian churches the concentration on the "Great Commandment" often has been interpreted as diminishing the relevance of the individual commandments of the Torah. But in spite of that, actual Christian ethics mainly has been built on the basis of the commandments of the Hebrew Bible. In particular, the Ten Commandments (Ex. 20, Deut. 5) are widely accepted, not only as the foundation of Christian ethics but even as a kind of "Magna Charta" for all humanity.

e) Justice and love often are taken as opposite to each other, similar to law and grace, characterizing the Jewish and Christian faith respectively. The Council of the Evangelical Church in Gemany (1975; *Doc. 14*), however, explained their inter-relation for both Jews and Christians:

> Christians and Jews are characterized in their self-understanding by the knowledge that they were chosen by God as partners to his covenant. In that election God reveals his love and his justice, from which grows the obligation for Jews and Christians alike, to work for a realization of justice and love in the world (I.5).

RR

4. Jesus

a) On this central issue, in contrast to the others which we have been examining, the problem with traditional Christian teaching has not been that of a hidden or open prejudice against and so a consequent misunderstanding of Jews or the Jewish tradition. The problem, rather, has been an almost total disregard of the Jewishness of Jesus and his whole context. As the author of a wholly new situation, Jesus could not, apparently, be thought of in solidarity with his past and with the traditions of his people: in effect, he could not be a Jew! Rather, for the main Christological tradition, Jesus, together with his family, friends, and disciples, and the scriptures to which he appealed, were extracted, as it were, from the tradition of his people and transposed into that of the church.

b) Only in recent decades has the recovery of the Jewishness of Jesus and of his context begun. In 1967, the Commission on Faith and Order could accept a report (*Doc. 4*) in which it was recognized that:

> (t)he first community of Christians were Jews...

and, without drawing a connection, the report pointed out that

> (i)n the realm of biblical scholarship there is today increasing cooperation among Christians and Jews.

Ten years later (*Doc. 15*), it was possible to recognize the Jewishness of Jesus more directly:

> Jesus was a Jew, "born of a Jewish mother" (II.1).

Further:

> The teaching of Jesus is rooted in Jewish thinking, in Jewish teaching and in Jewish life (II.2).

The same statement went on to point out that this insight had been gained in part from Jews:

> The meeting with Judaism helps Christians better to understand Jesus and his message (IV.2.b).

It should be recognized that while not all Jews have cared to participate in a Jewish reclamation of Jesus, the work of some Jews has helped to open Christian eyes to his Jewishness. This was acknowledged explicitly in the declaration of the Rhineland Synod of 1980 (*Doc. 17*, 2.4).

c) It is none the less true that little has been done to develop the Christological implications of the Jewishness of Jesus and his context. His Jewish identity and context are scarcely evident in the major Christological formulations of Nicea and Chalcedon. What follows from this new awareness? If Jesus is now to be confessed as a Jew, does that imply anything about the church's reading of the New Testament, in which we find witnesses both to his solidarity with and also to his estrangement from his people? If Jesus was a Jew in his life on earth, is he still a Jew? Is Jesus the same today as yesterday (Heb. 3:13)? If a modern epistemology insists that anything or anyone is understandable only within its context, what does that imply for the Christology of a church which acknowledges that Jesus was (is?) a Jew? Was not the church's classical Christology developed on the assumption that the church itself, not the Jewish people, was and is the context of Jesus Christ? The Bristol report (*Doc. 4*) had recognized that

> there is no doctrine of Christian theology which is not touched and influenced in some way by this confrontation with the Jewish people.

The fact remains that neither at Bristol nor in any of the documents of the intervening two decades has there been serious consideration of the implications of the church's growing awareness of the Jewishness of Jesus for the church's central Christological doctrine. The one sign that this problem will have to be addressed appears in the 1984 Guidelines of the Reformed Union of Germany, where it is pointed out that one of the errors, resulting from the early church's belief that it already possessed the fulfilment of the biblical promises, was that

> the human reality (*Menschsein*) of Christ was generalized into an abstract humanity (*zu einem abstrakten Menschenbild*).

d) From the medieval disputations up into the twentieth century, a recurring question in the relations between Christians and Jews has been, is Jesus the Messiah? The question was conceived to be a relatively simple one, admitting of only two possible answers: Christians said Yes, Jews said No, and therein was thought to lie the fundamental issue between them. The first statement of the WCC on the relationship between the church and the Jewish people (*Doc. 1*) stood squarely in this medieval heritage in asserting:

> We have... to proclaim to the Jews "The Messiah for Whom you wait has come."

By the time of Evanston, some recognition was made that the meaning of the term Messiah was not so simple in the first century, yet it was still assumed that there was one right meaning, the Christian one, and all the rest were false:

> at (Christ's) First Coming, the Jewish people had definite, if varied, Messianic hopes; and largely these hopes were inadequate or false, when "he came unto his own, his own received him not" (John 1:11) (*Doc. 2*).

This pattern was broken when a fundamental distinction of what Christ is for the Jewish people and for the church was noted in 1970 by the Synod of the Netherlands Reformed Church:

> Jesus Christ has a fundamentally different function for the nations and for Israel. The Jews are called back by him to the God who bound himself to them from their beginning. But the gentiles are not called back to their origins by Jesus Christ; rather, they are called to something which is radically new in their history (*Doc. 11*).

Beginning with the Declaration of the Rhineland Synod of 1980, there has begun to emerge a new note: the bond which Christ establishes between the church and the Jewish people, an important Christological development:

> We confess Jesus Christ the Jew, who as Israel's Messiah is the Saviour of the world and binds the peoples of the world to the people of God (4.3) (*Doc. 17*).

The Christological claim to which the churches have been coming in their recent statements, that in Christ God has bound the church to the Jewish people, is of primary importance, in our judgment. Whether the term Messiah is the best term with which to make the point is less clear. That term has seemed to ensure the connection between Jesus and the promises and witness of the Old Testament; can it be used without missionary overtones and without denying to the Jews the legitimacy of their own use of an important expression of their hope? The term preserves a political orientation recognized in liberation theology; can it be used without making Jesus the one who frees us from the "Jewish" law? The question confronting the church is whether it can find ways to make its foundational confession of faith in the Jew Jesus Christ as God's unique agent of life, reconciliation, and hope for the church, in such a way as also to make it clear that he is also God's confirmation of all God's promises to the Jewish people and thus the eternal bond between them and the church.

PvB

D. *Contemporary Theological Issues*

In modern times new problems arose that made the Christian attitude towards Jews and Judaism more complicated than it had been in traditional terms. Some of these problems had their roots in the earlier history of Christian-Jewish relations, as, for instance, with traditional antisemitism and Christian mission to the Jews. Others, such as difficulties arising from the creation of the State of Israel, appeared more recently. In most of these cases Christians are divided in their opinions and attitudes. Yet new approaches must be found in order to overcome the obstacles lying in the way of a renewal of Jewish-Christian relations. Most recently there is a growing awareness of a common responsibility Jews and Christians have for the world of today.

1. Antisemitism and Shoah

a) The term "antisemitism" came into use during the last decades of the nineteenth century when hatred and discrimination against Jews became an instrument in political and social struggles. Actually it was a modern social and political variant of anti-Judaism, which itself had its roots in the earliest beginnings of Christian history. This "contemporary" problem, then, has a long history. The statements of the World Council of Churches and its member churches show a growing awareness of these inter-relations.

b) Early Christian anti-Judaism had two different roots: (1) anti-Jewish elements existing in the pre-Christian world of the Roman empire (possibly Paul — or another writing in his name — used traditional pagan language to say that the "Jews displease God and oppose all men" [1 Thess. 2:15]); but (2) the major reasons for a negative and even hostile attitude by Christians towards Jews are to be found in the early development of Christianity itself.

For these latter two main reasons may be discerned. First:

> As Christianity came to define its own identity over against Judaism,... the church defined Judaism, and assigned to the Jews definite roles in its understanding of God's acts of salvation... in which they as a people are assigned to play a negative role (*Doc. 7*; 1.5).

Thus, in a certain sense anti-Judaism became an integral part of Christian self-definition.

> Tragically, such patterns of thought in Christianity have often led to overt acts of condescension, persecution, and worse (*Doc. 7*).

Second, this development had been strengthened decisively when in the fourth century C.E. Christianity entered into a coalition with political power. This is described in the Bristol report (1967; *Doc. 4*):

> After Christianity became the accepted religion of the Roman state, the Jews were discriminated against and often even persecuted by the "Christian" state, more often than not with ecclesiastical support (III).

c) Unfortunately it must be said that from that time on Jewish-Christian relations were characterized by discrimination, oppression, and too often even persecution of Jews by Christians. Many times pogroms and massacres occurred, some of them in close relation to particularly "Christian" events, such as the crusades in the eleventh to the thirteenth centuries.

The General Assembly of the Presbyterian Church (USA) (1987; *Doc. 20*) declared:

> In subsequent centuries... the church misused portions of the New Testament as proof texts to justify a heightened animosity towards Jews. For many centuries, it was the church's teaching to label Jews as "Christ-killers" and a "deicide race". This is known as the "teaching of contempt". Persecution of Jews was at times officially sanctioned and at other times indirectly encouraged or at least tolerated. Holy Week became a time of terror for Jews (5).

In many cases Jews were held responsible for disasters and epidemics, e.g. during the great pestilence in Europe in the fourteenth century, when Jews were accused of poisoning wells. Other stereotypical Christian accusations against the Jews, which often led to pogroms and massacres, included ritual murder of Christian children to drink their blood and desecration of eucharistic hosts. As a consequence of persecutions Jews often lost their homes and had to leave the countries where they lived. In several cases they were even officially expelled and banned by Christian monarchs, as in England (1290) and Spain (1492).

d) At the end of the eighteenth century a new chapter in the history of the Jews began. In the United States, since 1786 the small Jewish community had shared religious freedom with all other citizens. In Europe, the French revolution of 1789 opened the door to full civil rights for Jews as individuals in the modern secular state. But in the course of the nineteenth century new forms of social and cultural discrimination developed, which at the end of the century turned into modern antisemitism. Unfortunately, this new anti-Jewish movement adopted some of the most effective traditional Christian prejudices against the Jews, now merged with social and economic accusations of different kinds. Therefore antisemitism found a fertile soil among the traditional Christian population of European countries, though now more or less secularized, and even among the clergy and the members of the churches. Counter-forces within the society and the churches remained rather weak and without sufficient awareness of the dangerous developments.

A particularly fatal chapter began with the merger of antisemitism and the extreme right-wing fascist movement, primarily in Germany, which finally led to the attempt to exterminate the whole of European Jewry. It became evident that there were no forceful elements, either in the society or in the churches, that could have halted the progression into total political, moral, and (primarily) human disaster.

In 1948 the Bruderrat of the Evangelical Church in Germany[1] confessed:

> There was bound to be a bitter retribution for the fact that antisemitism rose and flourished, not only among the people (who still seemed to be a Christian nation), not only among the intelligentsia, and in governmental and military circles, but also among Christian leaders. And when finally this radical antisemitism, based on racial hatred, destroyed our nation and our churches from within, and released all its brutal force from without, there existed no power to resist it.

In 1987 the Presbyterian Church (USA) (*Doc. 20*) added, from a non-German perspective:

> It is disturbing to have to admit that the churches of the West did little to challenge the policies of their governments, even in the face of the growing certainty that the Holocaust was taking place.

e) After the end of the war, in February 1946, the Provisional Committee of the World Council of Churches (in Process of Formation)[2] expressed its

---

[1] See II.A.
[2] See III.B., note 1.

deep sense of horror at the unprecedented tragedy which has befallen the Jewish people in consequence of the Nazi attempt to exterminate European Jewry.

The First Assembly of the World Council (1948; *Doc. 1*) showed its consciousness of the Christian involvement in the development that led to these horror-full events:

> We have failed to fight with all our strength the age-old disorder of man which anti-semitism represents. The churches in the past have helped to foster an image of Jews as the sole enemies of Christ, which has contributed to anti-semitism in the secular world.

The Presbyterian Church (USA) (1987; *Doc. 20*) explained more explicitly the inter-relation between the teaching of the church and the Shoah:

> It is painful to realize how the teaching of the church has led individuals and groups to behavior that has tragic consequences. It is agonizing to discover that the church's "teaching of contempt" was a major ingredient that made possible the monstrous policy of annihilation of Jews by Nazi Germany (5).

A particular explanation of the way in which Christian thinking and teaching has contributed to antisemitism and its consequences is given by the Evangelical Church of the Rhineland (1980; *Doc. 17*):

> Throughout centuries the word "new" has been used against the Jewish people in biblical exegesis: the new covenant was understood as contrast to the old covenant, the new people of God as replacement of the old people of God. This obliviousness to the permanent election of the Jewish people and its relegation to non-existence marked Christian theology, church preaching and church work ever and again, right to the present day. Thereby we have also made ourselves guilty of the physical elimination of the Jewish people (4.7).

This thoughtful insight, that the denial of spiritual existence can lead to physical elimination, needs to be reflected upon further.

The Presbyterian Church (USA) (1987; *Doc. 20*) drew the following consequence of those insights:

> The church's attitudes must be reviewed and changed as necessary, so that they never again fuel the fires of hatred. We must be willing to admit our church's complicity in wrongdoing in the past, even as we try to establish a new basis of trust and communication with Jews. We pledge, God helping us, never again to participate in, to contribute to, or to allow the persecution or denigration of Jews, or the belittling of Judaism (5).

It has to be added that this demand for a review and, as far as necessary, changing of Christian theology is intended to lead to a renewed theology, which rightly could be called a "theology *after* the Holocaust (Shoah)"; there is no intention (as some critics suspect) of developing a "theology *of* the Holocaust".

RR

2. The State of Israel

a) Nothing in the church's tradition has prepared it for dealing with the State of Israel. Indeed, tradition has assumed as a matter of theological principle that a Jewish state was an impossibility: the Jews, we have taught, having rejected their Messiah and so their own inheritance, are condemned to wander the face of the earth in exile, until they turn to Christ or are confronted by him upon his return in glory. It is therefore not surprising that the churches have had difficulty in accounting for this new phenomenon, and that no consensus has yet arisen concerning the State of Israel. Furthermore, the absence of any analysis of the relationship between the Jewish people and the Land in all major documents of the WCC may be due to understandable apprehensions: fear of awakening eschatological fervour; aversion to the sacralization of any territory or institution; concern for the predicament of the Palestinians or of Christians in Arab or Islamic lands.

b) The First Assembly of the WCC expressed both bafflement, and also a haunting sense that more was involved than met the eye in the founding of the state: on the issue of conflicting "rights" in Israel, it said (1948; *Doc. 1*): "We do not undertake to express an opinion" on this, but they cautioned statesmen that in dealing with this difficult problem, they were confronted by "a moral and spiritual question that touched a nerve centre of the world's religious life".

On the other hand, the Faith and Order Bristol document showed some awareness of the importance of the State of Israel for Jewish faith, recognizing that the creation of the State "is of tremendous importance for the great majority of Jews" (1967; *Doc. 4*).

The first official church statement on the State of Israel that tried to go beyond this cautious "Yes, No, Maybe" was that of the General Synod of the Netherlands Reformed Church in 1970, which began by reasoning that the Jewish people today is the continuation of Israel, just as the church today is the continuation of the apostolic church, and then pointed out that the State of Israel is "one of the forms in which the Jewish people appear" (3). Having traced the ineradicable place of the Land in Israel's covenant with God, the Synod came to the far-reaching theological conclusion (*Doc. 11*):

> If the election of the people and the promises connected with it remain valid, it follows that the tie between the people and the land also remains by the grace of God (24).

The Synod granted that there is no biblical promise concerning the State, but in a section entitled, "The Relative Necessity of the State", it said:

> But as matters are at the moment, we see a free state as the only possibility which safeguards the existence of the people... Therefore we are convinced that anyone who accepts the reunion of the Jewish people and the Land for reasons of faith, has also to accept that in the given circumstances the people should have a state of their own.

c) The study of the Evangelical Church in Germany, "Christians and Jews", (1975; *Doc. 14*) was clear in recognizing the intimate bond between the people and the Land throughout Jewish history and traditions. On the subject of the state, it said:

> As a political entity, the State of Israel today has the form of a modern, secular state, organized as a parliamentary democracy... but such a characterization does not describe fully its significance: its name and founding documents place it expressly within Judaism's biblical traditions and thereby within the context of the history of the chosen people.

Christians consequently have "a duty" to recognize and support the UN resolutions enabling the Jews to live securely in their own state (III.3).

Similarly, the Central Board of the Swiss Protestant Church Federation in 1977, which saw the State of Israel as the fruit of a combination of ancient Jewish hope, nineteenth- and twentieth-century Zionism related to that hope, the UN resolution of 1947, and its having in fact become a place of refuge for Jews from all over the world, and having expressed deep concern for the situation of the Palestinians, went on to say (*Doc. 15*):

> We consider it the duty of the Christian churches and all Christians to intervene in defence of the right to existence of the Jewish people... and to stand by Israel in her growing isolation.

As for Jerusalem, the Board pointed out that the rights of all religious traditions, and respectful care of all holy places, have fared better under Israeli rule than under that of the Jordanians before them or that of the British under the Mandate.

The Rhineland Synod declaration of 1980 spoke of

> the continuing existence of the Jewish people, its return to the Land of Promise and the creation of the State of Israel as "signs of the faithfulness of God towards his people" (*Doc. 17*).

That view was reiterated by the Reformed Union of Germany (1984) in a statement that contains one of the most thoughtful theological insights to date: namely, that the return of the Jews to the Land is not only a confirmation of God's faithfulness, but one that recalls for Christians and all others "the earthly, historical dimension of God's promises".

The American Lutheran Church had found in 1974 that there was at that time no theological consensus on the relationship between the chosen people and the territory of the present State of Israel, and we suspect that this may be generally true still for most of the churches (see Chap. II.A). It identified three positions, which it called "a theology of the Land" (referring to such a position as that in Doc. 17,2.3); "a theology of the poor", in which concern for the plight of the Palestinians effectively prevents any favourable theological judgment concerning the State of Israel; and "a theology of human survival", which grants "juridical and moral grounds" for Christian support of the Jewish state (*Doc. 13*).

In 1979, the American Lutheran Church added:

> ...there is no consensus among Lutherans with respect to the relation between the "chosen people" and the territory comprising the present State of Israel. But there should be a consensus with respect to our obligation to appreciate, in a spirit of repentance for past misdeeds and silences, the factors which gave birth to the State of Israel...

The Swiss Protestant Church Federation revealed a similar lack of consensus. It said (1977; *Doc. 15*):

> Some Christians and many Jews see in the foundation of the State of Israel the fulfilment of the biblical promises. Others, among both Christians and Jews, regard it merely as a political deed which like every historical change entails political and human problems. The appreciation of the preservation of the Jewish people should determine our reflections between the two standpoints (VI.2).

In further reflection on the relative merits of both positions, and in the light of modest development since Amsterdam, the following points could serve as a minimum basis upon which a consensus might begin to be developed.

1. Because the State of Israel is in part the product of the ancient and living hope of the Jewish people and is of deep concern to almost all Jews, disregard for its safety and welfare is incompatible with concern for the Jewish people.

2. No degree of support for or theological validation of the State of Israel should imply, or be taken by others to imply, that all specific policies and actions of the Israeli government are beyond criticism. Here, however, a warning from the Synod of the Evangelical Church of Berlin (West) of 1984 is worth hearing (*Doc. 19*):

> Discussion among Christians would only be of any help at all to the persons concerned in Israel and the Near East in forming their political judgments, to the extent that the particular circumstances of the creation of the State of Israel, differences within Israeli society, and the difficulty of making judgments from outside, are all kept in mind (II.6).

3. Christian concern for the safety and survival of the State of Israel can in no way exclude Christian concern for the Palestinian people, and especially for Palestinian Christians of Israel and of the West Bank and Gaza. They, too, have a claim on the attention and concern of the church as to their situation, rights, and hopes. Christian concern for the legitimate rights of the Palestinians, however, may not annul Christian concern for Israel's legitimate right to live in safety.

4. Because God's covenant with the Jewish people has from its beginning been evidence of God's incarnate concern for the whole, concrete creation, the Jewish state is at the least a reminder of "the earthly, historical dimension of God's promises".

PvB

3. Mission to the Jews

As was pointed out in the chapter on the general trends in the World Council of Churches (II.A), the Consultation on the Church and the Jewish People of the World Council of Churches began its life as the Committee on the Christian Approach to the Jews, which was linked to the International Missionary Council until that Council was merged with the WCC in 1961. In the last decades a clear shift is visible in the documents of both the WCC and its member churches away from the missionary approach to the Jews towards a dialogical relationship between the church and the Jewish people.

a) In the statement received by the Amsterdam Assembly of the World Council (*Doc. 1*) entitled "The Christian Approach to the Jews", the WCC recommended that the churches

> seek to recover the universality of our Lord's commission by including the Jewish people in their evangelistic work;
> that in mission work among Jews they scrupulously avoid all unworthy pressures or inducements.

b) In the course of time the emphasis changed from mission to dialogue and there were even those, such as the framers of the Bristol report (*Doc. 4*), who argued that mission should be replaced by service:

> We all have to realize that Christian words have now become disqualified and suspect in the ears of most Jews. Therefore often the best, and sometimes even the only, way in which Christians today can testify to the Jewish people about their faith in Christ may be, not so much in explicit words, but rather by service.

Even those documents that insist on mission to Jews try to do so in a more differentiated way. Because sometimes dialogue is only viewed as another means for the missionary approach, it is necessary to formulate carefully what is meant by terms such as "mission" and "dialogue". Many statements and resolutions by churches and church bodies are ambivalent in this regard; much hesitation is evident, which reveals how difficult it is to speak in clear language about these terms.

The Council of the Evangelical Church in Germany tried, in its 1975 study, "Christians and Jews" (*Doc. 14*), to combine the concepts of "mission" and "dialogue":

> After all that has happened, there are many different opinions on the proper way of Christian witness. The discussion during the last few years has centred mainly on the terms "mission" and "dialogue"; these were often interpreted as mutually exclusive. We have now come to understand mission and dialogue as two dimensions of one Christian witness and this insight corresponds to the more recent view of Christian witness generally.

A consultation of the Lutheran World Federation [3] put it this way in 1982:

> In the same way that encounter with Judaism is significant for the church's "sentness" to the world, so also is the encounter with Jews important to Christians. Dialogue in an atmosphere of mutual respect should be pursued. Such dialogue may transform us with regard to our faith and calling; but it also includes a witness to Jesus Christ on our part.

---

[3] See III.A., note 1.

All the different attitudes and approaches towards mission to the Jews as described in the "Ecumenical Considerations" (1982; *Doc. 7*) are still present:

> There are Christians who view a mission to the Jews as having a very special salvific significance, and those who believe the conversion of the Jews to be the eschatological event that will climax the history of the world. There are those who would place no special emphasis on a mission to the Jews, but would include them in the one mission to all those who have not accepted Christ as their Saviour. There are those who believe that a mission to the Jews is not part of an authentic Christian witness, since the Jewish people finds its fulfilment in faithfulness to God's covenant of old.

c) Clear developments are discernible, however, in the direction of a more dialogical relationship between the church and the Jewish people, which are characterized by respect for each other's tradition. Proselytism as a zeal for converting others to one's own faith, which infringes upon the rights of human beings, is commonly rejected, as in the "Ecumenical Considerations":

> Steps towards assuring non-coercive practices are of highest importance. In dialogue ways should be found for the exchange of concerns, perceptions, and safeguards in these matters.

A distinction between mission on the one hand and the relation to the Jewish people on the other is made in the declaration of the Synod of the Rhineland (1980; *Doc. 17*):

> We believe in their calling Jews and Christians are always witnesses of God in the presence of the world and before each other. Therefore, we are convinced that the church may not express its witness towards the Jewish people as it does its mission to the peoples of the world.

A further step was taken by the Texas Conference of Churches (1982; *Doc. 18*). In the development of a new understanding between Jews and Christians, the Conference discovered the newest movement of the Spirit of God in our time:

> In reponse to this movement of the Holy Spirit today, we believe that the desired and most appropriate posture between Christians and Jews today is one of dialogue.

And then there is the statement by the Presbyterian Church (USA) in 1987 (*Doc. 20*), where we find the following on dialogue and mission:

Dialogue is the appropriate form of faithful conversation between Christians and Jews. Dialogue is not a cover for proselytism. Rather, as trust is established, not only questions and concerns can be shared but faith and commitments as well. Christians have no reasons to be reluctant in sharing the good news of their faith with anyone. However, a militancy that seeks to impose one's own point of view on another is not only inappropriate but also counterproductive.

d) The acceptance of a sincere dialogical relationship between Christians and Jews is still a matter of much debate in the churches. Those who are theologically and practically in favour of such a relationship base their motivation on several arguments:

Biblical: Romans 9-11 is often quoted as showing a certain tendency to acknowlege the continuity of the covenantal relationship between God and Israel until the end of time.

Historical: The situation of today differs fundamentally from that of the first century. The expected end of this age did not occur. The church became an almost totally gentile phenomenon, whereas in the first century there was a "church of the circumcision" next to a "church of the gentiles". Also the missionary situation is totally different. In the first century Jewish apostles became missionaries to the gentiles, but gentiles did not missionize Jews. Even in the Great Commandment (Matt. 28:16-20) the Jewish apostles are sent to the gentiles.

Theological: The Jewish people is still God's people, "beloved for the sake of their forefathers" (Rom. 11:28). Israel is still called by God to be God's witness before the nations of the world (Isa. 43:10). In this context an observation from the Bristol report (1967; *Doc. 4*) is significant:

If... the church is primarily seen as the people of God, it is possible to regard the church and the Jewish people together as forming the one people of God, separated from one another for the time being, yet with the promise that they will ultimately become one. Those who follow this line of thinking would say that the church should consider her attitude towards the Jews theologically and in principle as being different from the attitude she has to all other men who do not believe in Christ.

SSch

4. Common responsibility

a) Related to the new awareness of the common roots of the church and the Jewish people is the insight, expressed in several documents, that the commonalities are not restricted to the mutual relations of Jews and Christians but include a comon responsibility for the world of today. For instance, the Bristol report (1967; *Doc. 4*) reflected the challenge to Christian thinking from the Jewish concept of the world and humanity:

> The emphasis made by Jews in their dialogue with Christians on justice and righteousness in this world reminds the churches of the divine promise of a new earth and warns them not to express their eschatological hope one-sidedly in other-worldly terms.
>
> Equally, reflection in the light of the Bible on the Jewish concept of man as God's covenant-partner working for the sanctification of the world and for the bringing in of the kingdom should prompt the churches to reconsider their old controversy over the cooperation of man in salvation (V.4).

In the statement of the United Methodist Church (USA) (1972; *Doc. 12*) the first section on "Common Roots" is followed by a second one on "Service for Humanity". It begins:

> At this moment in history, the potential of our common heritage is particularly important for the advancement of causes decisive for the survival of all mankind. While it is true that the concept of human brotherhood and solidarity is not represented by Jews and Christians alone, this concept has been central for both from their beginnings. The sacredness of persons as God's creation is expressed clearly in both the Old and New Testaments The biblical view of each human being as an intrinsic member of the community of persons forbids any suppression of groups through society at large and manipulation of individuals as well.

This reminder of the concept of world and humanity in our common Bible is the point of departure for some more detailed reflections that are to be found in other documents.

b) The American Lutheran Church (1974; *Doc. 13*) declared in the preamble to its statement that:

> We need also to look to the future to see if there are things Christians and Jews can do together in service to the community. Better communication between Christians and Jews can lead to more adequate joint efforts on behalf of a humane society.

The Texas Conference of Churches (1982; *Doc. 18*) mentioned some particular common tasks:

> In particular, it is our belief that Jews and Christians share a common mission to work together in the accomplishment of these tasks:
> 1. The hallowing of God's name in the world.

2. Respect for the dignity and importance of the individual person as created in the image and likeness of God.
3. The active pursuit of justice and peace among and within the nations of the world.
4. To be a sign of hope in the future as promised by God.

The Evangelical Church in Germany (1975; *Doc. 14*) named among the "common roots" the inter-relations of justice and love (I.5). An explication of some consequences is given in the section on "Common Tasks" (III.5):

> Holy scripture, to which Jews and Christians refer their life, emphasizes the love of God for the disadvantaged and deprived. It is a task, then, for Christians and Jews to fight against the power of those who succeed and enrich themselves at the expense of the weak.

A key concept in these documents also appears in several other documents: the call for joint efforts on behalf of a humane society, including protest and struggle against any kind of oppression, exploitation, and persecution, with a particular emphasis on justice and peace. As the United Methodist Church stated explicitly (see D.4.1) this concern is not unique to Jews and Christians, but because it is a major theme of their common Bible, they have a common responsibility.

c) One of the areas where joint Jewish-Christian efforts towards justice and peace are particularly needed, of course, is in the Middle East conflict (see also D.2). The United Methodist statement includes a special section on "Responsibility in Problem Areas" (4) with the following observations:

> Dialogues presently are complicated by... turbulent political struggles such as the search for Jewish and Arab security and dignity in the Middle East. Facing these difficulties together may lead to creative results... In Jewish-Christian dialogues is placed a responsibility for being concerned for the implications in the Middle East for peace and justice for all persons.

Joint commitments by Christians and Jews are also asked for by the American Lutheran Church (see D.4.2). The Evangelical Church in Germany mentioned still another field, that of technology and ecology:

> The ever more apparent threat by technology to human existence makes it imperative to comprehend the world once more as a creation of God, to deal with it appropriately and according to the mandate received from God. That means that we turn away from a position in which man makes himself the measure of all things, exploits the world for his own good exclusively, and thereby becomes dependent on what he himself has produced.

d) The Bristol report discussed the inter-relation of eschatology and responsibility for the world (see D.4.1). Twenty years later the Presbyterian Church (USA) (1987; *Doc. 20*) came back to that aspect of the matter:

> Both Christians and Jews are called to wait and to hope in God. While we wait, Jews and Christians are called to the service of God in the world. However that service may differ, the vocation of each shares at least these elements: a striving to realize the word of the prophets, and attempt to remain sensitive to the dimension of the holy, an effort to encourage the life of the mind, and a ceaseless activity in the cause of justice and peace. These are far more than the ordinary requirements of our common humanity; they are elements of our common election by the God of Abraham, Isaac, and Jacob, and Sarah, Rebekah, Rachel, and Leah. Precisely because our election is not to privilege but to service, Christians and Jews are obligated to act together in these things. By so acting, we faithfully live out our partnership in waiting. By so doing, we believe that God is glorified.

RR

IV

Final Reflections

Almost forty years separate the statement on "The Christian Approach to the Jews" by the First Assembly of the World Council of Churches (*Doc. 1*) and "A Theological Understanding of the Relationship between Christians and Jews" by the newly-formed Presbyterian Church (USA) (*Doc. 20*). During those four decades the theology of the churches relative to the Jewish people has been debated in ways that could scarcely have been considered earlier. The debate has been erratic and sometimes acrimonious; sometimes welcomed and sometimes resisted. But it has gone on and continues to go on; and through it the churches are increasingly becoming aware that their own theological self-understanding is tied to the Jewish people.

These final reflections will attempt to highlight some, though by no means all, of the results produced by that awareness and, in particular, to suggest a few of the "next steps" that would seem to follow from the point at which the churches now are. It should be emphasized, however, that the churches in the Western world (from which the statements included in this study derive) are far from unanimous on most points and that churches in other parts of the world have, to date, felt little need to consider the Jewish people as a, much less the, central factor in their theological development.

A. Confession and geography

We who have worked on this report have been unable to discover official church statements concerning the Jewish people by the Orthodox churches or by Protestant churches outside the North Atlantic region. But we know from our own contacts with Christians in those churches and regions that there are sometimes strong feelings about Jews and Judaism and/or about the way Western European and American Christians and churches tend to understand their own relationship to the Jewish people. We realize that the specific history of the Western churches has been instrumental in shaping their theology. We would hope, however, to avoid the misunderstanding that stress on the particularity of Western church history neglects particularities present in other historical and geographical contexts, which may, in the days to come, bring important contributions to the development of church theology with reference to the Jewish people.

Many Christians in the Middle East, for instance, are unable to accept the positions taken by some European and American churches relative to such matters as the election of the Jewish people by God. As Canon Na'eem Ateek of St George's Cathedral (Anglican) in Jerusalem told the 1986 CCJP meeting:

> We have come to recognize that God is no longer the God of *Israel*. The problem is not only because I am a Palestinian — I am reflecting theology from my context — but from a larger perspective. I ask myself, Who said that God is the God of Israel? Is that what God says? Or is it what Israel says about God? At the heart of the discussion about election is our concept of God. From my understanding of faith in Christ, I am very uneasy with this concept of the God of *Israel*. That is a Jewish or an Israeli coinage, which looks at God and recognizes him to be *their* God — whereas the way I understand it is that God is the God who loved the world. God is the God of all people. I understand the Jewish origin, I recognize the Israel of God but, with Jesus Christ the *church* continues the line that began in the Old Testament. [1]

From Ghana, CCJP member Prof. Kofi Opoku [2] reflected in a similar vein:

> If God is seen as an electing God... it narrows down God's image, even though the concept of election was meant to enhance the image of God. On the contrary, it narrows it, particularly when we bear in mind the God who makes his rain to fall on the just and the unjust. When we bear in mind an African name for God which means, literally translated, "the plantain leaf large enough to shelter the entire world", we begin to get an idea of the kind of contrast the term "election" poses when it is associated with God. It seems to me that if we search for an image of God that... encourages openness, broad-mindedness, inclusiveness, outgoingness, we would come closest, at least humanly speaking, to a proper image of God.

---

[1] *Consultation on the Church and the Jewish People, Report*, Geneva, WCC, 1986, p.33.
[2] *Ibid.*, p.36.

These remarks clearly indicate that the theological understandings to which the World Council of Churches, through the Consultation on the Church and the Jewish People, [3] and some of its member churches have arrived are not necessarily shared by other Christians in the ecumenical movement who may live in social and political situations that differ from those prevailing across the North Atlantic. But, since their theology has not appeared in statements by official church bodies, we may only note it here. The instruction to the task force from the CCJP was to work at "distilling elements found in the various documents *already accepted* by various churches and the WCC itself". Thus we offer our theological comments to all the churches of the ecumenical movement as what they are — analyses based on the documents available from the churches and ecumenical councils that produced them.

B. Israel's covenant with God

The statements reproduced here, and the commentary on them, reveal that the World Council of Churches and many of its member churches have arrived at some rather certain theological positions resulting from almost forty years of dialogue and conscious interaction with the Jewish people. As such, they represent a major shift in the church's understanding of the Jewish people. Among these are that:
— the covenant of God with the Jewish people remains valid;
— antisemitism is "sin against God and man";
— coercive proselytism directed towards Jews is incompatible with Christian faith.

Although most frequently these theological positions are treated as discrete entities, they may most profitably be understood as flowing directly from the first fundamental affirmation: the covenant of God with the Jewish people remains valid.

The fact that Israel repeatedly is portrayed in the scriptures as having betrayed its side of the covenant demonstrates Israel's unfaithfulness, not God's. The record in the common scripture of Israel and the church reveals that, over and again, the prophets declared God as remaining faithful to the covenant, to which the people God chose as God's own are called to return. Now the churches in increasing numbers are agreeing with the prophets about the continuing validity of the covenant, in which the church has not replaced Israel. Generally speaking, however, the

---

[3] See Ecumenical Considerations on Jewish-Christian Dialogue (Doc. 7)

theological and ecclesiological implications of that acknowledgment have yet to be drawn out in official church documents. The churches — and, for that matter, most theologians — have scarcely begun to examine some extremely difficult questions arising from their "rediscovery" of God's faithfulness to the ancient covenant.

1. Ecclesiology

If the church did not replace Israel in the covenant with God — the Jewish people remaining God's people — how, then, are the churches to understand their own status vis-a-vis the God of Israel? The apparently simple affirmation of the covenant (which is received with applause by Jews and Jewish organizations) cannot for ever be left hanging without development of its ecclesiological implications.

Though they have rarely, if ever, made their way into the official theology of the churches, several solutions to this problem have been offered over the years. One is that God has entered into a "new covenant" with the church that stands alongside the covenant with Israel. This "two-covenant" theory has, however, been contested by those who would insist on a single covenant with two aspects, one Jewish, one Christian. Still another alternative has been to maintain that, since the covenant with Israel is the only covenant known through the scriptures, Christians and the church are somehow drawn into that covenant.

Since none of these has gained prominence in the churches' thinking, churches perhaps should focus their ecclesiological exploration of the implications of God's continuing covenant with the Jewish people by developing alternative ways of understanding the relationship between the church and the God known through the scripture and the New Testament. In so doing, they could avoid even the slightest suspicion that any trace of supersessionism, denied by acknowledgment of God's eternal faithfulness to the covenant with Israel, remains.

2. Antisemitism and Shoah

Christian complicity in the Shoah, confessed by a number of churches soon after the end of the war, forty years later was all but universally acknowledged by Western churches. As a consequence attention increasingly was paid to the history of Christian persecution of Jews from the beginning of the church. Although many in the churches rejected antisemitism prior to the Shoah, after it such rejection became the single most unambiguous element in ecclesiastical statements about Jews and Judaism.

The denunciation of antisemitism may be grounded in a type of theology that is different from the affirmation of the continuing validity of Israel's covenant with God. Antisemitism can be condemned on the ground that, since God loves all people, God loves Jews and, therefore, they must be honoured as part of the divine creation. But antisemitism is more than that; it is prejudice against and hatred for the Jewish *people*, which has resulted in pogroms over the centuries and, finally, the Shoah. Thus it is important for the churches to resist the temptation to think and act as though they had said everything there is to be said about antisemitism.

Because God remains in covenant with the people of Israel, antisemitism — hatred, persecution, prejudice against the Jewish people — is sin, which is to say conscious and intentional rejection of God. Though the declaration at the First Assembly of the World Council of Churches (*Doc. 1*) that "antisemitism is sin against God and man" has been repeated in other church statements, the fact that a major aspect of the sin described may be the church's usurpation of the covenant has seldom been recognized. But once the continuing validity of God's covenant with Israel is fully acknowledged, antisemitism may be seen to be direct attack upon God. In the next stage of the churches' theology that confession needs to be made explicit.

3. The nature of mission to the Jews

Fundamental shifts have occurred in the understanding of "mission to the Jews" during the period covered by this study. The churches remain uncertain, but increasingly they agree with the position reflected in the Bristol report (*Doc. 4*) that "the church should consider her attitude towards the Jews theologically and in principle as being different from the attitude she has to all other men who do not believe in Christ". The difference is the continuing covenant between God, whom Christians know through Jesus of Nazareth, and the Jewish people.

In the twentieth century a new phenomenon has emerged, largely as a result of missionary efforts to convert Jews to Christianity. "Hebrew Christians", believing their Christian faith not to be incompatible with status as part of the covenant people, attempt to be Jews and Christians at the same time, something that has not been a theological or ecclesiastical possibility since the church's decisive break with Judaism early in its history. The fact that Jews regard "Hebrew Christians" to be apostate needs to be taken into account when churches consider Christian mission to Jews, no less than the fact that the church today knows Christianity to be a distinctively different religion from Judaism.

Though a number of churches have denounced coercive proselytism, the next step may be to proscribe all proselytism of Jews on the theological ground that it is rejection of Israel's valid covenant with God.

* * *

In sum, those churches which incorporate the continuing reality of the covenant between the Jewish people and God into their official theology establish a premise with far-reaching implications, both for their relations with the Jewish people and for Christian theology itself. By and large, however, the development and implementation of those implications remain in the future.

AB